# Daily Prayer for All Seasons

CANTERBURY
PRESS
Norwich

© The Domestic and Foreign Missionary Society of
The Protestant Episcopal Church in the United States of America, 2014, 2016

First published by Church Publishing Incorporated
This Edition published in 2016 by Canterbury Press

Editorial office
Invicta House,
108-114 Golden Lane
London, EC1Y 0TG

Hymns Ancient & Modern® is a registered trademark of
Hymns Ancient and Modern Ltd.

Canterbury Press is an imprint of Hymns Ancient and Modern Ltd
(a registered charity)
13a Hellesdon Park Road, Norwich, Norfolk, NR6 5DR

www.canterburypress.co.uk

British Library Cataloguing in Publication data

Scripture from the New Revised Standard Version of the Bible, copyright ©1989,
Division of Christian Education of the National Council of the Churches of Christ in
the United States of America

Scripture quotations from THE MESSAGE. Copyright © by
Eugene H. Peterson 1993, 1994, 1995, 1996, 2000, 2001, 2001.
Used by permission of Tyndale House Publishers, Inc.

A catalogue record for this book is available
from the British Library

978 1 84825 898 3

Printed and bound by
CPI Group (UK) Ltd

# Contents

# Introduction

## Introduction

The Church has a deep, rich tradition of daily prayer, born in the desert, shaped in religious communities, developed in historic churches and lived out in countless Christian lives. It has been the bedrock upon which the Church has built its mission of worship, witness, pastoral care and commitment to social justice. Every revival in the history of the Church has been rooted in prayer. Every life transformed by the gospel has been fed by prayer.

Every major faith tradition has at its heart a daily rhythm of prayer. In the twenty-first century the Christian Church needs to own its treasures afresh so that we can enjoy the privilege of a prayerful day, punctuated by short but significant acts of graceful memory that put us back on track, returning the life-giving gaze of God.

This isn't about being unduly pious. It's simply re-orientating our lives to their Source, giving them a framework that holds them steady and true, whatever the external narrative of the day. What we find eventually is not so much that we are sustaining a life of prayer, as that God is sustaining us *through* a life of prayer. The great river of prayer and praise is forever rolling to the Ocean; we just, every so often, hop into a canoe.

If the Church of God has a problem it is that the practice of daily prayer has become unduly casual and perfunctory for many church-goers. Without prayer we cease to breathe as disciples of Christ; we develop 'heart failure'. And yet the treasure awaits. The diverse traditions of our spiritual pathways are prodigiously filled with inspiration and imagination. 'The one thing truly

worthwhile,' said Gregory of Nyssa, 'is becoming God's friend.'
And key to that aspiration is daily prayer.

All we have to do is to slow down and walk at the pace of
Love.

## Background

To greet the new millennium, the Church of England produced
new material for worship in its *Common Worship Services and
Prayers* (2000) and *Common Worship Daily Prayer* (2005). In
the latter there lies abundant material for seasonal services of
Morning and Evening Prayer and some material for Prayer
During the Day and for Compline. What is not provided –
because it was not requested – is a comprehensive sourcebook of
brief services modelled on the monastic 'hours', services helpfully
outlined on two or three pages and containing images, language,
poetry, meditations and prayers from across the whole
community of faith. This is the offer made by the present
volume, put together over a period of four years by a diverse
team of people from all over the United States, united in the
hope that their project would serve those both new to the
practice of prayer and those soaked in it yet wanting more.

In the life of prayer there is always 'more'.

+ John Pritchard

# About *Daily Prayer for All Seasons*

People in all kinds of religious traditions, including Judaism and Christianity, have been marking time with prayer for almost as long as we've had hours. "Praying the hours," as it's called, has always reminded us that God walks with us throughout each day; "praying the hours" is also a way that the community of faith comes together, whether we're all in one place or scattered like raindrops. Praying at set hours links us, both to God and to all God's people. We know this, and we are comforted.

*Daily Prayer for All Seasons* was compiled and written by a diverse team of people from all over the United States. We came together periodically over four years to create a set of prayers that acknowledge in their brevity both the need to pray and the short time we have to pray. The *Daily Prayer for All Seasons* team comprised people like you: we have jobs and families, groceries and gardens and ironing; subways to catch, doctors to see, and reports to write. We put these demands on the table. We never lost sight of those pressures on our time and energy as we plowed through wonderful resources for meditation and song, assembling the richest ones into a prayer book for all of us, clergy and laity, who think we're too busy to pray.

The consultants who compiled this book did so in prayer and with the hope that anyone — newcomer, stalwart, or someone in between — who wants to pray within the Christian tradition will be enriched by *Daily Prayer for All Seasons*. They are: Devon Anderson, Mark Bozutti-Jones, Rebecca Clark, Joseph Farnes, Paul Fromberg, Paul Joo, Lizette Larson-Miller, Julia McCray-Goldsmith, Sam Dessórdi Leite, Ernesto Medina, Clay Morris, Elizabeth Muñoz, Ruth Meyers, Dan Prechtel, Cristina Rose Smith, Carol Wade, Julia Wakelee-Lynch, Louis Weil.

# How to Use This Book

The church divides its calendar into periods called "seasons," which track the events of Jesus' birth, death and resurrection and the coming of the Holy Spirit to the Church. The seasons are Advent, Christmas, Epiphany, Lent, Holy Week (the final week of Lent), and Easter, followed by what the church calls Ordinary Time; because Ordinary Time is the longest season in the church year, we crafted two sets of services for the summertime: Creation (spiritual growth) and Rest. The eight sets of seasonal prayers provide the outer structure of *Daily Prayer for All Seasons*.

For the inner structure, each set of seasonal prayers falls into eight "hours," which follows the pattern of Benedictine monks, who divided the day into a cycle of eight intervals, called "hours," that effected a rhythm between work (*labora*) and prayer (*ora*). As a contemporary complement, the committee crafting *Daily Prayer for All Seasons* assigned a specific labour to each prayer "hour": We named dawn as the time for praise; we designated starting the day as the time for discernment; later morning, wisdom; midday, perseverance and renewal; afternoon, love; evening, forgiveness; bedtime, trust; and midnight we named as the time to watch. Each hour has a name, which also dates back to Christian monastic history and which we printed in italics after the hour's "work" name, for example, Praise (*Lauds*).

Don't be inhibited by the hours as we've labelled them. Maybe your day "starts" at the crack of noon or your bedtime comes after the night shift; maybe the end of your workday marks only the beginning of meetings for another part of your life. It's all right to adjust the prayers to the day as you live it, no matter how topsy-turvy it seems.

Adaptations for the prayers, lessons, meditations, and hymns may be made to suit the occasion. The questions that are provided for the meditations are only suggestions. They may be freely adapted, other questions may be used, or a period of silence may be kept.

# Format for the Hours

**BASIC FORM** (Praise, Watch): *Written in first person and generally anticipated for private use.*

**Entering** and **Going out (or Closing)**: the same simple, short call-and-response, which emphasizes the spiritual work of the hour

**Scripture**: a short, easily memorized passage, related to both the time and the season

**Meditation**: a question or a prompt for spiritual reflection

**Prayer**: a closing collect related to the hour and season

**SHORTER HOURS DURING THE DAY** (Wisdom, Perseverance and Renewal, Love, Trust): *Intended for group use, may be adapted for individual use.* These add the following to the basic form:

**Prayer**: an opening collect, suited to time and season

**Praise**: hymn, psalm, or canticle

**Meditation**: an inspirational quote precedes the prompt for reflection

**Prayers**: responsive prayers of the people, with space for personal intercession and thanksgiving

**Lord's Prayer:** Versions of the prayer are omitted to allow for local traditions; if praying in a group, the leader may choose to specify the form of the prayer (old/new, short/long, English/other language) to be used or encourage worshippers to pray in the language of the heart (versions of the Lord's Prayer appear in the Appendix).

**LONGER HOURS** (Discernment, Forgiveness): *Intended for group use, may be adapted for individual use.* To the above, add the following:

**Discernment:** affirmation

**Forgiveness:** confession and assurance of pardon (the latter allows for lay leadership of the hour whereas absolution requires a bishop or priest)

# Advent

The Christian calendar begins its new year not on January
1, but on the first Sunday of Advent — which is always four
Sundays before Christmas (December 25) and the Sunday
closest to St. Andrew's Day (November 30). Our word
"Advent" derives from the Latin *Adventus*, which means
"coming," and originally referred just to the coming of the
feast of Christmas. But over time the season of Advent took on
a double meaning. Today it refers both to the "first coming"
of Jesus Christ in his birth at Christmas and to his "second
coming" at the end of time.

It is important to remember that Advent is not just a season in
which we recall an event of the past — Jesus' birth — but also a
time in which we look to the present and the future. When will
Jesus come again? When will we see the kingdom of God on
earth, as it is in heaven? Of course no one knows. And so the
more important questions are: What can we do as the Church,
Christ's body here on earth, to welcome God's reign of justice
and peace today? What can we do as individuals to reorder our
lives in the light of God's love? What would it mean to live as a
people who believe in Jesus as the Saviour of all the earth and
who expect him to come again at the fulfillment of time? Each
Advent we turn to these questions anew. [1]

# Praise

*Lauds*        (Traditional hour: dawn/waking up)

Laudate, omnes gentes, laudate Dominum!
*[Sing praises, all people, sing praises to the Lord!]*
*We greet the new day by praising the Creator*
*(the ancient name for this hour, Lauds, means "praise").*

**Opening**        Praise the Lord, O my soul:
               **Praise God's holy name.**

**Scripture**      The glory of the Lord shall be revealed, and all
               people shall see it together.        Isaiah 40:5

**Meditation**  *How will I look for God's glory today?*
               *How will I help others see it?*

**Prayers**        Come, Emmanuel, come dwell with me.
               Hope of the world and Word of life:
               Come, Emmanuel, come dwell with me.

**Going Out**  Praise the Lord, O my soul:
               **Praise God's holy name.**

# Discernment

*Prime*          (Traditional hour: morning/start of the day)

*As we begin the day, we focus on our calling to live faithfully, for who knows what today holds?*

**Opening**     God's bright glory will shine,
                **and everyone will see it.**                    Isaiah 40:5 [2]

**Prayer**      O Holy One, thank you for coming to us anew this day. Prepare our hearts and reawaken our love for you as we discern your call within us. May we join with you in making level the path for all people. **Amen.**

**Praise**      *Prepare the way, O Zion*

                Prepare the way, O Zion, your Christ is drawing near!
                Let every hill and valley a level way appear.
                Greet one who comes in glory, foretold in sacred story.

                *Refrain*
                Oh, blest is Christ that came in God's most holy name.

                Words: Frans Mikael Franzen (1772-1847);
                tr. composite; adapt. Charles P. Price (1920-1999) [3]

**Scripture**   A voice cries out: "In the wilderness prepare the way of the LORD, make straight in the desert a highway for our God. Every valley shall be lifted up, and every mountain and hill be made low; the uneven ground shall become level, and the rough places a plain. Then the glory of the LORD shall be revealed, and all people shall see it together, for the mouth of the LORD has spoken."                    Isaiah 40:3-5

**Meditation** To enter Advent we leave fear for faith. Sam Portaro [4]

> *What fears must we release in order to level the way
> for ourselves and for others?*

**Affirmation**

> We believe in God, Creator of all:
>> The two-legged, the four-legged,
>> the winged ones, and those that crawl upon
>>> the earth
>> and swim in the waters.
> We believe in God, One Who Walked with Us:
>> Our Brother Jesus born in humility,
>> who lived and died for us and
>> who will come again to bring us to glory.
> We believe in God, Spirit with Us:
>> Ever present and ever guiding, upholding us and
>> showing us the principles to live by.
>> We hear God's voice through the prophets.
> Creator, One Who Walked with Us, Spirit with Us,
>> Holy One:
> We are named in the waters of baptism as your own,
> all of us related, all of us your children.
> We watch for signs of your homecoming
> and thank you for this sacred circle of life. Amen.

**Prayers**    In the beginning, it is dark, cool, and quiet,
               and we ask you:
**Invite us into your presence, O Christ.**
We do not know your works, Holy One,
               yet still we ask you:
**Invite us into your presence, O Christ.**
We look to the rising sun and trust that you
**invite us into your presence, O Christ.**

*Here, the people may add particular intercessions
or thanksgivings.*

You are our Shepherd, and we need nothing more.
We rejoice in your presence with us in all of creation.
               Amen.

**Lord's Prayer**

**Prayer**    God of hope, you call us from the exile of our sin
              with the good news of restoration;
              you build a highway through the wilderness;
              you come to us to bring us home.
              Comfort us with the expectation of your saving
              power, made known in Jesus Christ our Lord.
              **Amen.** [5]

**Going Out**  God's bright glory will shine,
               **and everyone will see it.**

5

# Wisdom

*Terce*     (Traditional hour: mid-morning)

*Having asked for direction and guidance, we pray now to equip ourselves properly for the journey ahead.*

**Opening**     All that we owe is redeemed
**in the love of God.**

**Prayer**     Wise and loving God, you bear us for joy. In humility, you show us wisdom. Enfold us at this hour with the knowledge born of love. Awaken within us the desire to know rightly and the will to live justly, with grace and generosity. **Amen.**

**Praise**     *A Song of True Motherhood*

God chose to be our mother in all things *
and so made the foundation of his work,
most humbly and most pure, in the
Virgin's womb.
God, the perfect wisdom of all *
arrayed himself in this humble place.
Christ came in our poor flesh *
to share a mother's care.
Our mothers bear us for pain and for death; *
our true mother, Jesus, bears us for joy and
endless life.
Christ carried us within him in love and travail, *
until the full time of his passion.
And when all was complete and he had carried us
so for joy, *
still all this could not satisfy the power
of his wonderful love.
All that we owe is redeemed in truly loving God, *
for the love of Christ works in us;
Christ is the one whom we love.

Julian of Norwich [6]

**Scripture**    A shoot shall come out from the stump of Jesse, and a branch shall grow out of his roots. The spirit of the Lord shall rest on him, the spirit of wisdom and understanding, the spirit of counsel and might, the spirit of knowledge and the fear of the LORD. He shall not judge by what his eyes see, or decide by what his ears hear; but with righteousness he shall judge the poor, and decide with equity for the meek of the earth.    Isaiah 11: 1-2, 4

**Meditation**    The desert is always the same, the sky is always beautiful, the road deserted....
The only thing that is always new is God.

Carlo Carretto [7]

*How will we ask for new eyes to see God and to see the needs in God's world?*

**Prayers**    Holy One, as we prepare for the advent of Christ,
**Give us your spirit of wisdom.**
As we seek to embody your love in the world,
**Give us your spirit of good counsel.**
As we seek to be faithful,
**Give us eyes to see beyond the obvious.**
As we gather in this hour, we lift all in need
before you.

*Here, the people may add particular intercessions or thanksgivings.*

May we be instruments of your peace on earth
**as we accept the gifts of your Spirit.**

**Lord's Prayer**

**Prayer**    God, whose holy name defies our definition but
whose will is known in freeing the oppressed:
Make us one with all who cry for justice, that we
who speak your praise may struggle for your truth;
through Jesus Christ. **Amen.** [8]

**Going Out**  All that we owe is redeemed
**in the love of God.**

# Perseverance and Renewal

*Sext*          (Traditional hour: mid-day)

*As we pause to feed our bodies in the middle of the day, we*
*pause also to feed our souls by vowing again to live faithfully.*

Opening          Do not be afraid.
                 **God is with us, always.**

Prayer           Shepherd of Israel, may Jesus, who is Emmanuel
                 and son of Mary, be more than just a dream in our
                 hearts. With the apostles, prophets, and saints,
                 save us, restore us, and lead us in the way of grace
                 and peace, that we may bear your promise into the
                 world. **Amen.** [9]

Praise           *The Song of Mary*  (Magnificat; Luke 1:46-55) [10]

                 My soul proclaims the greatness of the Lord,
                 my spirit rejoices in you, O God, my Saviour,
                     for you have looked with favor on your servant.
                 From this day all generations will call me blessed:
                     you, the Almighty, have done great things for me,
                     and holy is your Name.
                 You have mercy on those who fear you
                     from generation to generation.
                 You have shown strength with your arm
                     and scattered the proud in their conceit,
                 Casting down the mighty from their thrones
                     and lifting up the lowly.
                 You have filled the hungry with good things
                     and sent the rich away empty.
                 You have come to the help of your servant Israel,
                     for you have remembered your promise of mercy,
                 The promise made to our forebears,
                     to Abraham and his children for ever.

**Scripture**    When a woman is in labour, she has pain, because her hour has come. But when her child is born, she no longer remembers the anguish because of the joy of having brought a human being into the world. So you have pain now; but I will see you again, and your hearts will rejoice, and no one will take your joy from you.                        John 16: 21-22

**Meditation**    Ask yourself: Will this satisfy
a woman satisfied to bear a child?
Will this disturb the sleep
of a woman near to giving birth?                Wendell Berry [11]

*As we seek our own renewal, we look at others through the lens of compassion; how will this point of view affect our choices?*

**Prayers**    For our deepest and most holy longings we pray:
**Renew us, O God.**
For all who wander, who hunger, who thirst:
**Renew us as people of service and compassion.**
For this planet, our home:
**Renew our will to be healers of creation.**
For this and every nation:
**Renew in all people the will for good and
    the longing for peace.**
For those whom we hold in our hearts:

*Here, the people may add particular intercessions
or thanksgivings.*

Bless these and all creation with your goodness,
**and renew our trust in your love. Amen.**

**Lord's Prayer**

**Prayer**  O God of Elizabeth and Mary, you visited your
servants with news of the world's redemption in
the coming of the Saviour: Make our hearts leap
with joy, and fill our mouths with songs of praise,
that we may announce glad tidings of peace and
welcome the Christ in our midst. **Amen.** [12]

**Going Out**  Do not be afraid.
**God is with us, always.**

# Love

*As shadows lengthen, we are filled by the day's encounters; now, more than ever, we accept the depth and breadth of God's grace.*

**Opening**     In the beginning, God created, and it was good.
**In the beginning was the Word.**

**Prayer**      Creator of the world, you are the potter, we are the
clay, and you form us in your own image: Shape
our spirits by Christ's transforming power, that as
one people we may live out your compassion and
justice, whole and sound in the realm of your peace.
**Amen.** [13]

**Praise**      *O Come, thou Dayspring*

O come, thou Dayspring from on high,
and cheer us by thy drawing nigh;
Disperse the gloomy clouds of night
and death's dark shadow put to flight.
**Rejoice! Rejoice!**
**Emmanuel shall come again**
**and with us ever dwell.**

O come, Desire of nations,
bind in one the hearts of humankind;
Bid thou our sad divisions cease,
and be thyself our King of Peace.
**Rejoice! Rejoice!**
**Emmanuel shall come again**
**and with us ever dwell.**

**Scripture**     For the mountains may depart and the hills be
removed, but my steadfast love shall not depart from
you, and my covenant of peace shall not be removed,
says the Lord, who has compassion on you.

Isaiah 54:10

**Meditation**  Hail, Mary, full of grace.
The Lord is with you.
Blessed are you among women,
And blessed is the fruit of your womb, Jesus.

*How have we received love today, and how will we
bear its fruit to others?*

**Prayers**       God of compassion,
**Teach us to embody your love.**
God of faithfulness,
**Help us be constant in service.**
God of all creation,
**Give us compassion for all your children.**
God of blessing, hear our prayers.

*Here, the people may add particular intercessions
or thanksgivings.*

God of love,
**Draw our hearts to you.**

**Lord's Prayer**

**Prayer**        God of community, whose call is more insistent
than ties of family or blood: May we so respect
and love those whose lives are linked with ours
that we fail not in loyalty to you but make choices
according to your will. **Amen.** [14]

**Going Out**   In the beginning, God created, and it was good.
**In the beginning was the Word.**

# Forgiveness

*Vespers*     (Traditional hour: dusk/end of the day)

*As we turn on lamps at dusk, we greet the evening by welcoming God to abide with us anew.*

**Opening**     All who thirst
**come to the waters.**

**Prayer**     Holy One, whose coming we await, you invite
us into the light of your presence: Illumine the
dim places of our hearts. We are thirsty for your
compassion. Draw near to us and fill us, that we
may pour out your goodness to all who hunger.
**Amen.**

**Praise**     *A Song of the Spirit* (Revelation 22:12-17) [15]

"Behold, I am coming soon," says the Lord,
"and bringing my reward with me, *
     to give to everyone according to their deeds.
I am the Alpha and the Omega, the first and the last, *
     the beginning and the end."
Blessed are those who do God's commandments,
that they may have the right to the tree of life, *
     and enter the city through the gates.
"I, Jesus, have sent my angel to you, *
     with this testimony for all the churches.
"I am the root and the offspring of David, *
     I am the bright morning star."
"Come!" say the Spirit and the Bride; *
     "Come!" let each hearer reply!
Come forward, you who are thirsty, *
     let those who desire take the water of life as a gift.

**Scripture**    Ho, everyone who thirsts, come to the waters; and you that have no money, come, buy and eat! Come buy wine and milk without money and wisdom without price. Why do you spend your money for that which is not bread, and your labour for that which does not satisfy? Listen carefully to me, and eat what is good. Seek the Lord while he may be found, call upon him while he is near.    Isaiah 55:1-2a, 6

**Meditation**    Redemption is the journey of being reconnected to the light of God within. It is a journey home that takes us through what seems like unknown land. ... Redemption is not the bringing of light to a creation that is essentially dark, but rather the liberating of light from the heart of life.    J. Philip Newell [16]

*Where do we thirst for the light of redemption today? How will we offer that light to others who thirst?*

**Confession**    Most Holy God,
In the midst of this season of new life, we confess:
   We have resisted the light of your love;
   we have not fully shared the gifts entrusted
      to us; and
   we have not treasured the gifts of others around us.
   We stand in need of your love.
Holy Father, make us holy.
Holy Jesus, make us holy.
Holy Spirit, make us holy.
Holy God, make us whole. Amen. [17]

**Assurance of Pardon**

> God forgives us and loves us, and invites us
>> to continue the journey.
> As a woman is delivered from the pain of her
>> labour to the joy of cradling her child,
> **so are we delivered into God's grace.**

**Prayers**     Holy One, healer of the world,
**Shed your light upon this world.**
Holy One, healer of brokenness,
**Make us bold to share your light with others.**
Holy One, healer of the world, we offer
our prayers:

*Here, the people may add particular intercessions
or thanksgivings.*

Lead us to wholeness
**And make us shine with your light of healing love.**

**Lord's Prayer**

**Prayer**     God, our healer, whose mercy is like a refining fire:
Touch us with your judgment and confront us with
your tenderness; that, being comforted by you, we
may reach out to a troubled world; through Jesus
Christ. **Amen.** [18]

**Going Out** All who thirst
**come to the waters.**

# Trust

*Compline* (Traditional hour: night/bedtime)

*We sum up this day with a bedtime prayer to examine our conscience and offer our actions to God.*

**Opening**  Be strong and let your heart take courage, **all you who wait for the Lord.** Psalm 31:24

**Prayer**  Holy One, whose coming we await, we lift our hearts to you: Remind us of your faithfulness, that we may trust ever more deeply in your grace. We set down the tasks of the day so that we may arise renewed, to love and serve you. **Amen.**

**Praise**  *The Song of Hannah* (1 Samuel 2:1-2,8) [19]

My heart exults in you, O God; *
   My triumph song is lifted in you.
For I rejoice in your salvation: *
   There is none holy like you.
God raises the poor from the dust; *
   And lifts the needy from the ash heap
To make them sit with the rulers *
   and inherit a place of honor.
For the pillars of the earth are God's *
   on which the whole earth is founded.

**Scripture**  The Spirit of the Lord is upon me, because the Lord has anointed me; he has sent me to bring good news to the oppressed, to bind up the brokenhearted, to proclaim liberty to the captives, and release to the prisoners; and to proclaim the year of the Lord's favor. Isaiah 61:1-2a

**Meditation** *A Reflection on Finding your Way:*
*What To Do in the Darkness*

> Go slowly
> Consent to it
> But don't wallow in it
> Know it as a place of germination
> And growth
> Remember the light
> Take an outstretched hand if you find one
> Exercise unused senses
> Find the path by walking in it
> Practice trust
> Watch for dawn
>
> Marilyn Chandler McEntyre [20]

*How shall we travel through the darkness of*
*Advent?*

**Prayers** God of grace and hope:
**Help us to move from fear to trust.**
Your grace surrounds and fills us:
**Remind us that you provide all we need.**
Your healing love is offered to all:

*Here, the people may add particular intercessions*
*or thanksgivings.*

May we be full of peace in our waiting
**And full of joy in our praise of you. Amen.**

**Lord's Prayer**

**Prayer** Merciful God of peace, your word, spoken by the
prophets, restores your people's life and hope:
Fill our hearts with the joy of your saving grace,
that we may hold fast to your great goodness and
proclaim your justice in all the world. **Amen.** [21]

**Closing** Be strong and let your heart take courage,
**all you who wait for the Lord.** Psalm 31:24

# Watch

*Vigils*          (Traditional hour: late night)

*Like nuns and monks at prayer, we can listen in the stillness of the night to hear God's call.*

**Opening**      Even in the waiting,
                 **God is with me.**

**Scripture**    The true light, which enlightens everyone,
                 was coming into the world.          John 1:9

**Meditation**   *What keeps me in the shadows?*
                 *What light am I waiting for?*

**Prayers**      Holy One, come this night.
                 Open my heart to the brightness of your love.
                 Release my fears and revive my hope,
                 that I may rest well and rise to share your love.
                 **Amen.**

**Closing**      Even in the waiting,
                 **God is with me.**

# Christmas

For the church, Christmas is a time to celebrate the birth of Jesus in Bethlehem. We celebrate this birth not because Jesus was simply a "good man" but because we believe Jesus was — and is — both the human son of Mary and the divine Son of God. That makes Christmas a time to reflect on a mystery that the church calls the doctrine of the Incarnation. This important theological term comes from the Latin word *carne,* which means "flesh," and has to do with the divine taking on human flesh and coming among us in human form.

In one of his Christmas sermons Augustine, the fifth-century bishop of Hippo, described the mystery of the Incarnation this way: "Beloved, our Lord Jesus Christ, the eternal creator of all things, today became our Saviour by being born of a mother. Of his own will he was born for us today, in time, so that he could lead us to his Father's eternity. God became human like us so that we might become God. The Lord of the angels became one of us today so that we could eat the bread of angels."

# Praise

*Lauds*        (Traditional hour: dawn/waking up)

Laudate, omnes gentes, laudate Dominum!
*[Sing praises, all people, sing praises to the Lord!]*
*We greet the new day by praising the Creator*
*(the ancient name for this hour, Lauds, means "praise").*

**Opening**    Praise God from the heavens;
               **sing praise in the heights!**

Psalm 148:1 [22]

**Scripture**  The people who walked in darkness have seen
               a great light.                          Isaiah 9:2

**Meditation** *Where will I seek God's light today?*

**Prayers**    Open my eyes this day, dear Lord, to see
                    your light in the world.
               Accompany me, so that I may walk faithfully
               and share the light of your love with others. **Amen.**

**Closing**    Praise God from the heavens.
               **Sing praise in the heights!**

# Discernment

*As we begin the day, we focus on our calling to live faithfully, for who knows what today holds?*

**Opening**     The Word made flesh
                **makes God known to us.**

**Prayer**      Light of life, you came in flesh, born into human
                pain and joy, and gave us power to be your
                children: Grant us faith, O Christ, to see your
                presence among us, so that all creation may sing
                new songs of gladness and walk in the way of
                peace. **Amen.** [23]

**Praise**      *The Song of Mary*   (*Magnificat*; Luke 1:46-55) [24]

                My soul proclaims the greatness of the Lord,
                    my spirit rejoices in you, O God, my Saviour, *
                    for you have looked with favor on your servant.
                From this day all generations will call me blessed: *
                    you, the Almighty, have done great things for me,
                    and holy is your Name.
                You have mercy on those who fear you *
                    from generation to generation.
                You have shown strength with your arm, *
                    and scattered the proud in their conceit,
                Casting down the mighty from their thrones *
                    and lifting up the lowly.
                You have filled the hungry with good things *
                    and sent the rich away empty.
                You have come to the help of your servant Israel, *
                    for you have remembered your promise of mercy,
                The promise made to our forebears, *
                    to Abraham and his children forever.

**Scripture**    And the Word became flesh and lived among us, and we have seen his glory, the glory as of a father's only son, full of grace and truth. From his fullness we have all received grace upon grace. No one has ever seen God. It is God the only Son, who is close to the Father's bosom, who has made God known.

*John 1:14, 16, 18*

**Meditation**    You will know when it is time to bring to birth the new creation. The signs will be all around you, urging, insisting: Now is the time. You have to know just when to bear down and concentrate on one thing only. It takes labour, hard, hard labour to bring to birth something new.

*Miriam Therese Winter* [25]

*What is God calling forth from us? How will we labour to birth what God calls for?*

**Affirmation**

We believe in God, the source of love,
  who created humanity in God's own image
    and likeness,
  who blessed them and asked them to
  procreate, nurture and preserve God's creation
    for prosperity.
We believe in Jesus Christ, God incarnate,
  who was born of a woman and was a carpenter,
  who identified himself with women, men
    and children,
    transforming them to have life abundantly.
We believe in the Holy Spirit active before creation,
  who through the ages has inspired Christians
    without number,
  who continues to inspire us to usher in the reign
    of God,
  where no one is cast out, lonely or bereft. [26]

23

**Prayers**   Wonderful Counselor,
whose glory is beyond our understanding
and whose love is beyond measure:
**Let us know your presence now.**

Mighty God,
whose power girds creation,
whose hands cradle the hills, yet whose mercy is
    boundless:
**Let us know your presence now.**

Prince of Peace,
whose righteousness is like the strong mountains
and whose justice is as the great deep:
**Let us know your presence now.**

Emmanuel,
whose property it is always to have mercy,
and whose arm is long to save, we lift before you now:

*Here, the people may add particular intercessions
or thanksgivings.*

Hold all those we love in your unbounded love.
**Make us your healing presence in the world.** [27]

**Lord's Prayer**

**Prayer**   Loving Word of God, you have shown us the
fullness of your glory in taking human flesh: Fill us,
in our bodily life, with your grace and truth, that
our pleasure may be boundless and our integrity
complete. **Amen.** [28]

**Going Out**   The Word made flesh
**makes God known to us.**

# Wisdom

*Terce*  (Traditional hour: mid-morning)

*Having asked for direction and guidance, we pray now to equip ourselves properly for the journey ahead.*

**Opening**  O come, all ye faithful.
**Come, let us adore him.**

**Prayer**  O holy Wisdom: Fill us this day with joy,
understanding and grace, that we may tell out the
wonder of your love; through Christ our Lord. **Amen.**

**Praise**  *Go Tell It on the Mountain*

*Refrain:*
 Go tell it on the mountain, over the hills
  and everywhere.
 Go tell it on the mountain, that Jesus Christ is born.

While shepherds kept their watching o'er
 silent flocks by night,
behold throughout the heavens there shown
 a holy light.  *Refrain*

The shepherds feared and trembled, when lo!
 above the earth,
Rang out the angel chorus that hailed the
 Saviour's birth.  *Refrain*

Down in a lowly manger the humble Christ was born,
and God sent us salvation that blessed
 Christmas morn.  *Refrain*

Words: John W. Work Jr.

**Scripture**    But when the fullness of time had come, God sent his Son, born of a woman, born under the law, in order to redeem those who were under the law, so that we might receive adoption as children. So you are no longer a slave, but a child, and if a child, then also an heir, through God.    Galatians 4:4-5, 7

**Meditation**  We who are charged with announcing the message of Christ need to learn the incomparable lesson that he taught us by his own example. He taught first of all with his life, and only then did he preach.

Dom Helder Camara [29]

*What are we called to preach with our lives today?*

**Prayers**    Holy Wisdom, you fill us with goodness,
        and we are grateful:
    **Let us show with our lives.**
    Holy Wisdom, you invite us to serve,
        and we answer "yes":
    **Let us show with our actions.**
    Holy Wisdom, you open our eyes to those in need,
        and we want to be faithful:
    **Let us show with our love.**
    Holy Wisdom, we want to live more deeply in
        your peace:
    **Show us the Way.**

    *Here, the people may add particular intercessions
    or thanksgivings.*

**Lord's Prayer**

**Prayer**    Great Spirit, God, Creator of all, we receive you into our hearts, our minds, our Souls: Grant us Mary's wisdom to heed the inner voice that we know is you. Guide us to accept your invitation to serve and to do so with strength and courage. **Amen.**

**Going Out**    O come, all ye faithful.
**Come, let us adore him.**

# Perseverance and Renewal

*Sext*       (Traditional hour: mid-day)

*As we pause to feed our bodies in the middle of the day, we pause also to feed our souls by vowing again to live faithfully.*

**Opening**     All life is interwoven.
                 **All life is gift from God.**

**Prayer**      Giver of life and author of love: Be present at this hour as we pause to rest in your love. Fill us with the memory of your goodness, bless us with the grace of your light, and send us out again with renewed faithfulness to show your love to the world. **Amen.**

**Praise**      *Love Came Down at Christmas*

Love came down at Christmas,
Love all lovely, love divine;
Love was born at Christmas:
Star and angels gave the sign.

Worship we the Godhead,
Love incarnate, love divine;
Worship we our Jesus,
But where for a sacred sign?

Love shall be our token;
Love be yours and love be mine,
Love to God and neighbour,
Love for plea and gift and sign.

Words (alt.): Christina Rossetti

**Scripture**   But when the goodness and loving-kindness of God our Saviour appeared, he saved us, not because of any works of righteousness that we had done, but according to his mercy, through the water of rebirth and renewal by the Holy Spirit.            Titus 3: 4-5

**Meditation**  Grace is often portrayed as "washing away" the things that obscure the essential goodness of life. That light that was in the beginning still glows at the heart of life, but we do not see its full brilliance. ... Grace is like a cleansing rain over the landscape of life, followed by a sunlight that restores our vision.            J. Philip Newell [30]

*Where do we need the grace of renewal right now? How can we offer it to others?*

**Prayers**   God our Saviour,
**Cleanse from our hearts all that impedes your love.**
God our Saviour,
**Renew in us the desire to live in your grace.**
God our Saviour,
**Fill us again with the will to persevere.**
God our Saviour, we bless your name and ask
     your healing love:

*Here, the people may add particular thanksgivings and intercessions.*

Give us ever-grateful hearts,
**To share your love with all.**
Hold all the earth in your goodness,
**And make us ministers of your gospel.**

**Lord's Prayer**

**Prayer**    God of creation, through your great mercy you
renew us: Send us now back to the love and labour
of this day with joy and compassion in our hearts;
Through Christ our Saviour. **Amen.**

**Going Out**    All life is interwoven.
**All life is a gift from God.**

# Love

*None*      (Traditional hour: afternoon)

*As shadows lengthen and we are filled by the day's encounters,
we accept again the depth and breadth of God's grace.*

**Opening**      Little One, born this day:
            **Saviour, Redeemer, Beloved of God.**

**Prayer**      Blessed Saviour, in love you came to us as a child:
            Enlighten our hearts, that we may more deeply
            understand the richness of this gift and practice
            more faithfully your call to give of ourselves in love.
            **Amen.**

**Praise**      *Shengye quing, shengye jing/*
            *Holy Night, Blessed Night*[31]

            *Refrain*:
                Holy night, blessed night.

            Stars shine brightly, earth is still,
            Hills and valleys, field and woodlands,
            all surround the small town Bethlehem.
            In a manger Christ the Lord sleeps.  *Refrain*

            Angels sing praise, shepherds fear,
            Earth and heaven ring with praises,
            "Alleluia" all creation sings
            Tell the good news: Christ is born now.  *Refrain*

            Christ has come down, dwells with us.
            Sacrifice, love, peace, and justice
            shine upon us like the morning sun.
            Grace and glory bless the whole world.  *Refrain*

**Scripture**  As God's chosen ones, holy and beloved, clothe yourselves with compassion, kindness, humility, meekness and patience. Bear with one another and, if anyone has a complaint against another, forgive each other; just as the Lord has forgiven you, so you must also forgive. Above all, clothe yourselves with love, which binds everything together in perfect harmony. Let the peace of Christ rule in your hearts, [and] let the word of God dwell in you richly.                    Colossians 3:12-15a, 16a

**Meditation**  Let us imagine that within us is an extremely rich place, built entirely of gold and precious stones. … [W]ithin us lies something incomparably more precious than what we see outside ourselves. Let's not imagine that we are hollow inside.
                    Theresa of Avila [32]

*What does it mean that God's love dwells in us?*
*How might this help us love others?*

**Prayers**  Beloved, we are called to love those in need:
**Let us love in truth and action.**
Beloved, we are called to be people of peace:
**Let us love one another.**
Beloved, we are called to be people of healing:
**Let us love not only God, but our brothers**
      **and sisters, also.**

*Here, the people may add particular intercessions*
*or thanksgivings.*

May we abide in God's love.
**May God's love abide in us.** [33]

**Lord's Prayer**

**Prayer**     Saviour, Redeemer, Beloved of God: Clothe us in
               your love, strengthen us to live gently on this earth,
               give us humility to see all we encounter as precious
               to you, and teach us to walk with kindness and
               patience this hour and always. **Amen.**

**Going Out**  Little One, born this day:
               **Saviour, Redeemer, Beloved of God.**

# Forgiveness

*Vespers*     (Traditional hour: evening/end of the day)

*As we turn on lamps at dusk, we greet the evening by welcoming God to abide with us anew.*

**Opening**   The light shines in the darkness,
**and the darkness has not overcome it.**

**Prayer**    God our Saviour: Meet us in this time and place;
focus our hearts on your love, feed the hungry
places of our souls, release us from all that resists
your grace, and renew our bodies to serve your
world. **Amen.**

**Praise**    *Hark! the Herald Angels Sing*

Hark! the herald angels sing
Glory to the newborn King!
Peace on earth and mercy mild,
God and sinners reconciled!
Joyful, all ye nations rise,
Join the triumph of the skies;
With the angelic host proclaim
Christ is born in Bethlehem!

*Refrain:*   Hark! the herald angels sing
Glory to the newborn King!

Words (alt.): Charles Wesley

**Scripture** The true light, which enlightens everyone, was
coming into the world. He was in the world, and
the world came into being through him; yet the
world did not know him. He came to what was his
own, and his own people did not accept him. But
to all who received him, he gave power to become
children of God.                    John 1:9-12

**Meditation** Holiness is not an attainment, in any sense of the term, but is a gift of the Word of God. Holiness is not a badge of achievement for a saint, but is wrought in the life, in the very being, of an ordinary person by the will of the Word of God. Holiness ... is the restoration of integrity and wholeness to a person. William Stringfellow [34]

*What do we, needing wholeness, present to God at this hour?*

**Confession** Word of God,
we confess that we need your wholeness.
We have often looked to outward gifts
and measures
when what we need is your love in our hearts.
We have often aimed toward what we can achieve
or where we stand in relation to others,
when what we desire is the integrity your love
bestows.
We confess our need for your illumination.
Be our light, O Christ.

**Assurance of Pardon**
God forgives all our sins
and heals all our infirmities.
God lifts us from the low places
and sets mercy and love upon us.
God fills us with goodness
and renews our lives.
Thanks be to God. [35]

**Prayers**     For all who are oppressed,
**May we proclaim the justice of God's Kingdom.**
For all who hunger,
**May we, the Body of Christ, be bread.**
For all who weep,
**May we offer comfort and joy.**
For all who are outcast or in any need or trouble:

*Here, the people may add particular intercessions
or thanksgivings.*

As we yearn to be the faithful people of God,
**May we be people of true and gracious welcome
    to all.** [36]

**Lord's Prayer**

**Prayer**     O God, who wonderfully created, and yet more
wonderfully restored, the dignity of human nature:
Grant that we may share the divine life of him who
humbled himself to share our humanity, your Son
Jesus Christ; who lives and reigns with you, in the
unity of the Holy Spirit, one God, for ever and ever.
**Amen.** [37]

**Going Out**  The light shines in the darkness,
**and the darkness has not overcome it.**

# Trust

*Compline*   (Traditional hour: night/bedtime)

*We sum up this day with a bedtime prayer to examine our conscience and offer our actions to God.*

**Opening**   Jesus the Word
**now dwells among us.**

**Prayer**   Almighty and ever-loving God, you have poured
upon us the new light of your incarnate Word:
Grant that this light, enkindled in our hearts, may
shine forth in our lives; through Jesus Christ our
Lord. **Amen.**[38]

**Praise**   *O Little Town of Bethlehem*

O little town of Bethlehem, how still we see thee lie!
Above thy deep and dreamless sleep, the silent stars
   go by;
yet in thy dark streets shineth the everlasting Light;
the hopes and fears of all the years are met in thee
   tonight.

For Christ is born of Mary; and gathered all above,
while mortals sleep, the angels keep their watch of
   wondering love.
O morning stars, together proclaim the holy birth!
and praises sing to God the King and peace to all
   on earth.

How silently, how silently, the wondrous gift is
   given!
So God imparts to human hearts the blessings of his
   heaven.
No ear may hear his coming, but in this world of sin,
where meek souls will receive him, still the dear
   Christ enters in.

Where children pure and happy pray to the blessed
    Child,
where misery cries out to thee, Son of the mother
    mild;
where charity stands watching and faith holds wide
    the door,
the dark night wakes, the glory breaks, and
    Christmas comes once more.

O holy Child of Bethlehem, descend to us, we pray;
Cast out our sin and enter in, be born in us today.
We hear the Christmas angels the great glad tidings
    tell;
O come to us, abide with us, our Lord Emmanuel!

Words: Phillips Brooks (1835-1893)

**Scripture**   O God, you will keep in perfect peace those whose
minds are fixed on you; for in returning and rest we
shall be saved; in quietness and trust shall be our
strength.                                    Isaiah 26: 3, 30:15

**Meditation** The frightened shepherds become God's messengers.
They organize, make haste, find others, and speak
with them. Do we not all want to become shepherds
and catch sight of the angels?
I think so. ...Because the angels sing, the shepherds
rise, leave their fears behind, and set out for
Bethlehem, wherever it is situated these days.

Dorothy Soelle [39]

*As we lay aside the concerns and fears of this day,*
*where do we need strength and courage to tell*
*God's good news to others tomorrow?*

**Prayers**     Jesus the Word,
**We pray for the confidence of your peace in our lives.**
Jesus the Word,
**We pray for all those who live amid violence or uproar.**
Jesus the Word,
**We pray for the earth, knowing we have broken its peace.**
Jesus the Word,
**We pray for all those in need of good news this night:**

*Here, the people may add particular intercessions or thanksgivings.*

With the angels and shepherds that first Christmas,
**O Jesus, the Word made flesh,**
may we trust in and share the joy of your incarnation.

**Lord's Prayer**

**Prayer**     Gracious God, you have redeemed us through Jesus Christ, the firstborn of all creation, whose birth we celebrate as the child of Bethlehem: Bless us with every spiritual blessing, that we may live as your adopted children and witness to your glory with unending praise and thanksgiving. **Amen.** [40]

**Closing**    Jesus the Word
**now dwells among us.**

# Watch

*Vigils*        (Traditional hour: late night)

*Like nuns and monks at prayer, we can listen in the stillness of the night to hear God's call.*

**Opening**     O come, let us worship
**Christ the Lord.**

**Scripture**   For a child has been born for us ... and he is named
Wonderful Counselor, Mighty God, Everlasting
Father, Prince of Peace.                    Isaiah 9:6

**Meditation** *How is Jesus my counselor, loving parent, strength and/or peace this night?*

**Prayers**    Fill us, gentle God, with so great a sense of you in
our souls that we never know abandonment, never
know despair. Lead us beyond ourselves to become
what you were born to be. Never let us be deterred
by those who burden us with false expectations. In
your holy name, we pray. **Amen.** [41]

**Closing**    O come, let us worship
**Christ the Lord.**

# Epiphany

*Epiphany* is a Greek word meaning "manifestation, showing forth, revelation." This feast proclaims our faith that in Jesus, God is revealed to all people — not just to an inner circle or a chosen few, but to all people, in all places, and throughout all time. Christians believe that in the person of Jesus we see who God is, and in the words and actions of Jesus we see God at work in the world. Epiphany marks a series of occasions at which Jesus was revealed to be God's Son.

The feast of Epiphany and the weeks that follow are a time when we reflect on several "manifestations" of Jesus, as he was recognized as the Messiah (or Christ) by many different people. We hear about Jesus' baptism in the river Jordan by John the Baptist and the visit of the magi, or wise men, who followed the star to Bethlehem at Jesus' birth. We share the amazement of the guests at the wedding party at Cana as Jesus performs his first miracle by turning water into fine wine. And at the end of the season we see Jesus' glory shown to three of his disciples on the mountain as he is transfigured before them in a blaze of light.

# Praise

*Lauds*          (Traditional hour: at dawn/waking up)

Laudate, omnes gentes, laudate Dominum!
*[Sing praises, all people, sing praises to the Lord!]*
*We greet the new day by praising the Creator*
*(the ancient name for this hour, Lauds, means "praise").*

**Opening**      Arise, shine, for your light has come.
**And the glory of the Lord has dawned upon you.**

**Scripture**    God said, "Let there be light," and there was light.
And God saw that the light was good.          Genesis 1:3

**Meditation**   *How will I invite God's love to shine through me*
*today?*

**Prayer**       Brightest and best of the stars of the morning,
Dawn on our darkness and lend us thine aid;
Star of the east, the horizon adorning,
Guide where the infant Redeemer is laid.

**Going Out**    Arise, shine, for your light has come.
**And the glory of the Lord has dawned upon you.**

# Discernment

*Prime*      (Traditional hour: morning/start of the day)

*As we begin the day, we focus on our calling to live faithfully, for who knows what today holds?*

**Opening**      Your word is a lamp to our feet
**and a light for our path.**

**Prayer**      Insistent God, by night and day you summon
your slumbering people: So stir us with your voice
and enlighten our lives with your grace that we
give ourselves fully to Christ's call to mission and
ministry. **Amen.** [42]

**Praise**      *Psalm 27:1, 5-6, 10-11* [43]
God is my light and my salvation;
      whom then shall I fear?
God is the strength of my life;
      of whom then shall I be afraid?
One thing have I asked of you, O God;
      one thing I seek:
      that I may dwell in your house all the days of
            my life,
To behold your fair beauty, O God,
      and to seek you in your temple.
Hearken to my voice, O Most High, when I call;
      have mercy on me and answer me.
You speak in my heart and say, "Seek my face."
      Your face, O God, will I seek.

**Scripture**      The next day, John again was standing with two of
his disciples, and as he watched Jesus walk by, he
exclaimed, "Look, here is the Lamb of God!" The
two disciples heard him say this, and they followed
Jesus. When Jesus turned and saw them following,
he said to them, "What are you looking for?"
John 1:35-38

**Meditation** The eye of the cormorant is emerald. The eye of the eagle is amber. The eye of the grebe is ruby. The eye of the ibis is sapphire. Four gemstones mirror the minds of birds, birds who mediate between heaven and earth. We miss the eyes of the birds, focusing only on feathers. Terry Tempest Williams [44]

*What are we looking for? Where have we failed to look?*

**Affirmation**

We are not alone; we live in God's world.
We believe in God:
    who has created and is creating,
    who has come in Jesus,
    the Word made flesh,
    to reconcile and make new,
    who works in us and others by the Spirit.
We trust in God.
We are called to be the Church:
    to celebrate God's presence,
    to live with respect in creation,
    to love and serve others,
    to seek justice and resist evil,
    to proclaim Jesus, crucified and risen,
    our judge and our hope.
In life, in death, in life beyond death, God is with us.
We are not alone. Thanks be to God. [45]

**Prayers**　Jesus, you are the light of the world:
**May your light open our eyes to see those in need.**
Jesus, you are the light of the world:
**May the works of our lives demonstrate your love.**
Jesus, you are the light of the world:
**May your wisdom enlighten our decisions.**
Jesus, you are the light of the world,
　　hear the prayers of our hearts:

*Here, the people may add particular intercessions
or thanksgivings.*

As you enlighten our lives,
**May we be light for others.**

**Lord's Prayer**

**Prayer**　Open our eyes that we may see.
Incline our hearts that we may desire.
Order our steps that we may follow
the way of your commandments. **Amen.** [46]

**Going Out**　Your word is a lamp to our feet
**and a light for our path.**

# Wisdom

*Terce*        (Traditional hour: mid-morning)

*Having asked for direction and guidance, we pray now to equip
ourselves properly for the journey ahead.*

**Opening**    Wisdom knows and understands all things
               **and guides us in our actions.**

**Prayer**     O God, your Spirit of Wisdom was present at the
               creation and with Jesus at his baptism: Open our
               hearts to that same Spirit, and strengthen and
               guide us to love and serve you and our neighbours;
               through Jesus Christ our Lord. **Amen.**

**Praise**     *A Song of the Spirit of Wisdom*   (Wisdom 7:7-8, 10-14a) [47]
               I prayed and understanding was given me; *
                   I called on God and the Spirit of Wisdom came
                       to me.
               I preferred her to scepters and thrones, *
                   and I accounted wealth as nothing in comparison
                       with her.
               I loved her more than health or beauty, *
                   and I chose to have her rather than light
                   because her radiance never ceases.
               In her company, all good things came to me; *
                   in her hands, a wealth of true riches.
               In all these good things, I rejoiced
                   because Wisdom brings them, *
                   but I did not know that she was their mother.
               What I learned without selfishness I pass on
                       without reserve; *
                   I do not hide her gifts.
               For Wisdom is an unfailing treasure for mortals: *
                   those who receive her are friends with God.

**Scripture**   Who is wise and understanding among you? Show by your good life that your works are done with gentleness born of wisdom. ... The wisdom from above is first pure, full of mercy and good fruits, without a trace of partiality or hypocrisy. And a harvest of righteousness is sown in peace for those who make peace.                   James 3:13, 17-18

**Meditation**   Do not think that saintliness comes from occupation; it depends rather on what one is. The kind of work we do does not make us holy, but we may make it holy.              Meister Eckhart (1260-1329)

*What work will we do today?*
*How will we make it holy?*

**Prayers**   Breath of God, inspire us with your guidance.
   **Come to us, Holy Spirit, and be present with us.**
Wisdom of God, guide us to works of goodness
      and mercy.
   **Come to us, Holy Spirit, and be present with us.**
Spirit of God, teach us to be faithful.
   **Come to us, Holy Spirit, and be present with us.**

*Here, the people may add particular intercessions or thanksgivings.*

**Lord's Prayer**

**Prayer**   Gracious God: give us deeper reverence for the truth and such wisdom in the use of knowledge that your kingdom may be advanced and your name glorified;through Jesus Christ our Lord. **Amen.** [48]

**Going Out**   Wisdom knows and understands all things,
   **and she will guide us in our actions.**

# Perseverance and Renewal

*Sext*        (Traditional hour: mid-day)

*As we pause to feed our bodies in the middle of the day, we pause also to feed our souls by vowing again to live faithfully.*

**Opening**     We long for glory.
**Transform us with your glory.**

**Prayer**      Holy One, you know our needs before we ask:
Grant that we may persevere in our prayers for the
needs of all creation, and renew our trust in your
loving care for us; through Jesus Christ our Lord.
**Amen.**

**Praise**      *Songs of Thankfulness and Praise*

Songs of thankfulness and praise,
Jesus, Lord to you we raise,
manifested by the star
to the sages from afar;
branch of royal David's stem
in your birth at Bethlehem;
anthems be to you addressed,
God in flesh made manifest.

Manifest in Jordan's stream,
Prophet, Priest, and King supreme;
and at Cana, wedding guest,
in your Godhead manifest;
manifest in power divine,
changing water into wine;
anthems be to you addressed,
God in flesh made manifest.

Words (alt.): Christopher Wordsworth (1807-1885)

**Scripture**   On the third day there was a wedding in Cana of Galilee. ... When the wine gave out, the mother of Jesus said to him, "They have no wine." And Jesus said to her, "Woman, what concern is that to you and to me? My hour has not yet come." His mother said to the servants, "Do whatever he tells you." ... Jesus said to them, "Fill the jars with water." [The water became wine.] Jesus did this, the first of his signs, in Cana of Galilee, and revealed his glory; and his disciples believed in him.   John 2: 1-5, 7-11

**Meditation**   In the name of God, stop a moment, close your work, look around you.   Leo Tolstoy [49]

*What can we let go this hour, and how will it free us to use our gifts with greater joy?*

**Prayers**   When we labour and are laden with worries
                 and cares,
        **Refresh us, O Christ.**
   When our hands are not ready to accept help,
        **Renew our trust, O Christ.**
   When we grow weary of loving others,
        **Love us, O Christ.**
   We offer you the cares of our hearts:

   *Here, the people may add particular intercessions or thanksgivings.*

   As we lift our hopes and joys to you,
        **Hear us, O Christ. Amen.**

**Lord's Prayer**

**Prayer**　　O God of steadfast love, at the wedding in Cana, your Son Jesus turned water into wine, delighting all who were there: Transform our hearts by your Spirit, that we may use our gifts to show forth the light of your love as one body in Christ. **Amen.** [50]

**Going Out**　We long for glory:
　　　　　　**Transform us with your glory.**

# Love

*None*     (Traditional hour: afternoon)

*As shadows lengthen, we are filled by the day's encounters; now, more than ever, we accept the depth and breadth of God's grace.*

**Opening**     Beloved, we are called to be your children:
**May we delight in your love.**

**Prayer**     God, you draw us into your love through baptism:
Teach us to abide in the knowledge of your love
and to share that love with all your creation;
through Jesus Christ our Lord. **Amen.**

**Praise**     *You, O Christ* [51]
You, O Christ, are the One: *
    the might and goodness of fatherhood.
You are the One:*
    the wisdom and kindness of motherhood.
You, O Christ, are the One:
    the light and grace of all blessed love; *
    you are Trinity; you are Unity.
You, O Christ, are the One; *
    the high sovereign goodness of all manner of
        things.
You are the One who makes us to love;*
    you are the One who makes us to long.
You, O Christ, are the One: *
    the endless fulfilling of all our true desires.

**Scripture**     When Jesus had been baptized, just as he came up
from the water, suddenly the heavens were opened
to him, and he saw the Spirit of God descending
like a dove and alighting on him. And a voice from
heaven said, "This is my Son, the Beloved, with
whom I am well pleased."     Matthew 13:15-17

**Meditation** I was suddenly overwhelmed with the realization that I loved all those people, that they were mine, and I theirs, that we could not be alien to one another even though we were total strangers. It was like waking from a dream of separateness. ...

Thomas Merton [52]

*How would our day be different if we could see every person as God's beloved child?*

**Prayers** God our Creator and Lover,
**Fill our hearts with your love.**
God our Saviour and Lord,
**Fill our home with your love.**
God our Sustainer and Advocate,
**Fill our community with your love.**
God the Holy Trinity,
**Fill all the world with your love.**

*Here, the people may make particular intercessions and thanksgivings.*

**Lord's Prayer**

**Prayer** O God most holy, in Jesus Christ you have laid a foundation upon which to build our Lives: Help to follow your perfect law of love, that we may fulfill it and observe it to the end. **Amen.** [53]

**Going Out** Beloved, we are called to be your children:
**May we delight in your love.**

# Forgiveness

*Vespers*      (Traditional hour: evening/end of the day)

*As we turn on lamps at dusk, we greet the evening by welcoming God to abide with us anew.*

**Opening**      The Saviour of the nations has come,
              **To light our way and heal our wounds.**

**Prayer**      Set us free, O God, from the bondage of our sins,
              and give us the liberty of that abundant life, which
              you have made known to us in your Son, our
              Saviour Jesus Christ; who lives and reigns with you,
              in the unity of the Holy Spirit, one God, now and
              for ever. **Amen.**

**Praise**      *Many Are the Light Beams / Muchos Resplandores* [54]

              Many are the light beams from the one light.
                  Our one light is Jesus.
              Many are the light beams from the one light;
                  we are one in Christ.

              *Muchos resplandores, sólo una luz;*
                  *Es la luz de Cristo.*
              *Muchos resplandores, sólo una luz;*
                  *Que nos hace uno.*

              Many are the branches of the one tree.
                  Our one tree is Jesus.
              Many are the branches of the one tree:
                  we are one in Christ.

              *Muchas son las ramas, un árbol hay,*
                  *y su tronco es Cristo.*
              *Muchos son las ramas, un árbol hay,*
                  *y en el somos uno.*
              Words: Anders Frostenson (1906-2006); trans.: Pablo Sosa (b.1933)

**Scripture** On entering the house, they saw the child with Mary his mother; and they knelt down and paid him homage. Then, opening their treasure chests, they offered him gifts of gold, frankincense, and myrrh. And having been warned in a dream not to return to Herod, they left for their own country by another road.                    Matthew 2:11-12

**Meditation** The wise men cannot return to their own country by the same way they used to come to Bethlehem. While they cannot go the same route because of Herod, we cannot go the same way once we have met Christ. We emerge from our encounter with Christ as changed people. We cannot follow the same path as before. Like the wise men, we must seek out Christ, but we will always leave as transformed people.                    Richard Meux Benson [55]

*Where do we seek transformation? Where do we need to offer another way to someone else?*

**Confession** Holy One, we encounter you in our lives and try to follow faithfully,
**but so often we get lost or turn away.**
We try to love our neighbours and ourselves,
**and even, by your grace, to love our enemies,**
**but we fail.**
We take the wrong path and stray from the way of your love.
**Forgive us, Lord, and guide us back to you.**

**Assurance of Pardon**
**We turn to you, God of Love, and**
**we accept your grace.**
**We accept your pardon.**
**We accept the gift of a new path,**
**through Christ our Lord. Amen.**

**Prayers**    Among the lowly you were born.
**Lord Jesus, save us.**
The wise and powerful bowed down before you.
**Lord Jesus, teach us.**
You have come to lead us to holiness.
**Lord Jesus, guide us.**
You ask us to call on you, and so we offer these
prayers:

*Here, the people may make particular intercessions
and thanksgivings.*

**Lord Jesus, hear us.**

**Lord's Prayer**

**Prayer**    Jesus, you revealed yourself to the world so that
all people might look to you and be saved: may we
know the wholeness that you bring. Be our light in
the darkness that we may not stumble, and lift us
up again if we fall; all this we ask in your name.
**Amen.**

**Going Out**    The Saviour of the nations has come
**to light our way and heal our wounds.**

# Trust

*Compline*    (Traditional hour: night/bedtime)

*We sum up this day with a bedtime prayer to examine our conscience and offer our actions to God.*

**Opening**    Do not fear, for I have redeemed you.
**You call us by name, and we are yours.**

**Prayer**    O God of all the prophets, you knew us and chose us before you formed us in the womb: Fill us with faith that speaks your word, hope that does not disappoint, and love that bears all things for your sake, until that day when we shall know you fully, even as we are known by you. **Amen.** [56]

**Praise**    *The Song of Simeon* (*Nunc dimittis*; Luke 2: 29-32) [57]
Lord, you now have set your servant free *
    to go in peace as you have promised;
For these eyes of mine have seen the Saviour, *
    whom you have prepared for all the world to see:
A Light to enlighten the nations, *
    and the glory of your people Israel.

**Scripture**    Six days later, Jesus took with him Peter and James and his brother John and led them up a high mountain, by themselves. And he was transfigured before them, and his face shone like the sun, and his clothes became dazzling white. ... Suddenly a bright cloud overshadowed them, and from the cloud a voice said, "This is my Son, the Beloved; with him I am well pleased; listen to him!" When the disciples heard this, they fell to the ground and were overcome by fear. But Jesus came and touched them, saying, "Get up and do not be afraid."

Matthew 17:1-2, 5-8

**Meditation** *Candelmas*

With certitude
Simeon opened
ancient arms
to infant light.
Decades
before the cross, the tomb
and the new life,
he knew
new life.
What depth
of faith he drew on,
turning illumined
towards deep night.

Denise Levertov [58]

*How will we let go of fear and draw on our faith as Simeon did?*

**Prayer** Son of God, in the light of faith, we offer our prayers:
**May we follow closely your lead.**
For all who face the darkness with fear this night,
**Redeem our fears with hope and confidence.**
For all the places in this world that yearn for new life,
**Grant the light of your saving grace.**
For all the joys and concerns of our hearts:

*Here, the people may offer particular intercessions and thanksgivings.*

Hear us, teach us, restore us,
**And may your light shine in our hearts and in all the world.**

**The Lord's Prayer**

**Prayer**     Be our light in the darkness, O Lord, and in your
               great mercy defend us from all perils and dangers
               of this night; for the love of your only Son, our
               Saviour Jesus Christ. **Amen.** [59]

**Closing**    Do not fear, for I have redeemed you.
               **You call us by name, and we are yours.**

# Watch

*Vigils*          (Traditional hour: late night)

*Like nuns and monks at prayer, we can listen in the stillness of the night to hear God's call.*

**Opening**    Darkness is not dark to you;
                     **the night is as bright as the day.**

**Scripture**   O tarry, and await God's pleasure; be strong,
                     and let your heart take comfort;
                     Wait patiently for God.                    Psalm 27:18 [60]

**Meditation** *How does God's faithfulness sustain me?*
                     *How do I remain faithful?*

**Prayer**      Guide us waking, O God,
                     and guard us sleeping,
                     that, awake, we may watch with Christ,
                     and, asleep, we may rest in peace. **Amen.** [61]

**Closing**     Darkness is not dark to you;
                     **the night is as bright as the day.**

# Lent

Figuring out how to keep a holy Lent can be a challenge, but if we move beyond the popular conceptions (and misconceptions), Lent holds the possibility for real change — or to use the church's word, conversion — in our lives, as well as for rich and lasting spiritual growth. (The word "lent" comes from the Anglo-Saxon word *lencton*, referring to the springtime of the year when the days grow longer and warmer and brighter.)

Lent emerged in our history as a season of final preparation for those who would be baptized at the Great Vigil of Easter. The entire Christian community was highly invested in walking alongside those who were about to commit their lives to Christ. In time, the season took on some extra layers of meaning, and many people now associate it with listening for a deeper awareness of our own sin — how we fall short of the ideals God sets before us — and the need for ongoing repentance and amendment of life.

That said, joy in the new life we have found in the Christian faith should never be overwhelmed by our struggles to live out that faith or our awareness of the ways we fall short. We can see Lent as an opportunity to deepen our spiritual lives. In Lent we step back and consider the ways we need to repent, to turn around — to be converted.

During Lent we as individual Christians and as a church — the Body of Christ — consider our spiritual health. How are we living the gospel in our lives, our homes, our churches, our towns, our schools, our places of work? What areas of growth or signs of renewal should we celebrate with gratitude and joy? In what ways have we fallen short, grown stagnant or cold-hearted, or failed to love God by embracing new life when we encounter it? These are the kinds of questions we ask ourselves during the weeks of Lent.

# Praise

*Lauds*     (Traditional hour: at dawn/waking up)

Laudate, omnes gentes, laudate Dominum!
*[Sing praises, all people, sing praises to the Lord!]*
*We greet the new day by praising the Creator*
*(the ancient name for this hour, Lauds, means "praise").*

**Opening**     Bless the Lord,
            **O my soul.**

**Scripture**     O God, you are my God; eagerly I seek you.

Psalm 63:1 [62]

**Meditation** God has given to the earth the breath that feeds it.
            God's breath vibrates in yours, in your voice. It is
            the breath of God that you breathe.

Theophilus of Antioch [63]

            *How will God breathe through me this day?*

**Prayer**     Lord, you beat in our hearts and thrive in every cell
            of our bodies.
            All that we are leaps for delight. Wherever we go,
            we know we shall find you there. **Amen.** [64]

**Going Out** Bless the Lord,
            **O my soul.**

# Discernment

*Prime*          (Traditional hour: morning/start of the day)

*As we begin the day, we focus on our calling to live faithfully, for who knows what today holds?*

**Opening**      Show our hearts your way,
                 **and we shall follow.**

**Prayer**       O God of love, you are the true sun of the world,
                 evermore risen and never going down: We pray you
                 to shine in our hearts and drive away the darkness
                 of sin and the mist of error. We pray that we
                 may, this day and all our lives long, walk without
                 stumbling in the way you have prepared for us,
                 which is Jesus Christ our Lord; who lives and reigns
                 with you and the Holy Spirit, one God in glory
                 everlasting. **Amen.** [65]

**Praise**       *Lead Me, Guide Me*

                 Lead me, guide me along the way,
                 for if you lead me, I cannot stray.
                 Lord, let me walk each day with thee.
                 Lead me, O Lord, lead me.

                 I am lost if you take your hand from me,
                 I am blind without thy light to see.
                 Lord, just always let me thy servant be.
                 Lead me, O Lord, lead me.

                 Lead me, guide me along the way,
                 for if you lead me, I cannot stray.
                 Lord, let me walk each day with thee.
                 Lead me, O, Lord, lead me.

                 Words and Music: Doris Akers (1923-1995) [66]

**Scripture**   Is not this the fast that I chose: to loose the bonds
of injustice, to undo the thongs of the yoke, to let
the oppressed go free, and to break every yoke? Is it
not to share your bread with the hungry, and bring
the homeless poor into your house; when you see
the naked, to cover them, and not to hide yourself
from your own kin? Then shall your light break
forth like the dawn, and your healing shall spring
up quickly; your vindicator shall go before you, the
glory of the Lord shall be your rear guard. Then
you shall call, and the Lord will answer; you shall
cry for help, and he will say, "Here I am."

Isaiah 58:6-9a

**Meditation**   We live in a time of struggle between truth and lies,
between sincerity, which almost no one believes in
still, and hypocrisy and intrigue. Let's not be afraid,
brothers and sisters; let's try to be sincere, to love
truth; let's try to model ourselves on Christ Jesus. It
is time for us to have a great sense of selection, of
discernment.                           Oscar Romero [67]

*How will we practice Christ Jesus' way of love,
justice, and truth this day?*

**Affirmation**

We believe that Jesus took the form of a slave,
    so we commit ourselves to serve others.
We believe that God is love,
    so we commit ourselves to reconciliation.
We believe that Jesus gives us his Spirit,
    so we commit ourselves to his work in the world.
We believe that God is the light of life,
    so we commit ourselves to bearing God's light
        in our world.
We believe that the Spirit speaks through us,
    so we commit ourselves to proclaim the good
        news of abundant life in the world God loves.

**Prayers**  Loving God, in our faith, we pray:
For reconciliation between the violated and
the violent,
**That we may rest in your peace.**
For generosity between rich and poor people
everywhere,
**That we may share the abundance of your
creation.**
For the growth of love between broken peoples
and nations,
**That we may shape our common life as your
kingdom.**
For mutual respect between immigrants and
insiders,
**That we may welcome your image in all who
come to us.**
For protection for the weak and humility for
the strong,
**That we may serve others as you serve us in
Christ.**

*Here, the people may add particular intercessions
or thanksgivings.*

For all the joys and concerns of our hearts,
**That we may live with gladness and trust.**

**Lord's Prayer**

**Prayer**  Heavenly Father, in you we live and move and have
our being: We humbly pray you so to guide and
govern us by your Holy Spirit, that in all the cares
and occupations of our life we may not forget you,
but may remember that we are ever walking in your
sight; through Jesus Christ our Lord. **Amen.** [68]

**Going Out**  Show our hearts your way,
**and we shall follow.**

# Wisdom

*Terce*       (Traditional hour: mid-morning)

*Having asked for direction and guidance, we pray now to equip ourselves properly for the journey ahead.*

**Opening**  Know the grace of God
**and live joyfully this day of salvation.**

**Prayer**   God of heaven and earth, your wisdom stretches
around the world, ordering all things for good:
Free us from anxiety and understand us like a
friend, that we might share the good news of your
friendship with all people; through the Word made
flesh, Jesus Christ, our Lord. **Amen.**

**Praise**   *Come, heavenly comforter*
Come, heavenly comforter
     and spirit of truth,
Blowing everywhere
     and filling all things.
Treasury of blessings
     and giver of life:
Come and abide in us;
     cleanse us from every impurity,
     and, in your great goodness, save us. [69]

**Scripture** As we work together with Christ, we urge you not
to accept the grace of God in vain. For he says, "At
an acceptable time I have listened to you, and on a
day of salvation I have helped you." See, now is the
acceptable time; see, now is the day of salvation!

2 Corinthians 6:1-2

**Meditation** We can all please God. We must only choose well. Many go abroad to study, pursuing knowledge far from home, but the kingdom of God is always here and now, wherever you are, within you. Precisely because the kingdom is within, and God is our friend, our salvation only requires that we be willing.                                    Athanasius of Alexandria [70]

*In what ways are we willing to accept the wisdom of God's guidance today?*

**Prayers**

Christ in my mind
    **that I may see what is true;**
Christ in my mouth
    **that I may speak with power;**
Christ in my heart
    **that I may learn to be loved;**
Christ in my hands
    **that I may work with tenderness;**
Christ in my soul
    **that I may know my desire;**
Christ in my arms
    **that I may reach without fear;**
Christ in my face
    **that I may shine with God.** [71]

*Here, the people may add particular intercessions or thanksgivings.*

**Lord's Prayer**

**Prayer**　　Wisdom is brilliant; she never fades. By those who love her, she is easily seen; by those who seek her, she is readily found. She is a breath of God's power, an image of God's goodness, the eternal light and mirror of God's glory. Now let Wisdom do all things, renew all things, and pass into holy souls everywhere to make them friends of God.  **Amen.** [72]

**Going Out**　Know the grace of God
**and live joyfully this day of salvation.**

# Perseverance and Renewal

*Sext*        (Traditional hour: mid-day)

*As we pause to feed our bodies in the middle of the day, we
pause also to feed our souls by vowing again to live faithfully.*

**Opening**     Renew and strengthen us, eternal God,
**as we prepare for resurrection.**

**Prayer**      Merciful God, your strength and courage pour
forth to sustain the witness of your faithful people:
Awaken in us the humility to serve wherever
creation is broken and needy, that we may follow
in the way of our brother, Jesus, die as he did to
all that separates us from you, and be raised, as he
was, to new life. **Amen.** [73]

**Praise**      *A Song of the Wilderness*  (Isaiah 35:1-4) [74]
The wilderness and the dry land shall be glad, *
    the desert shall rejoice and blossom;
It shall blossom abundantly, *
    and rejoice with joy and singing.
They shall see the glory of the Lord, *
    the majesty of our God.
Strengthen the weary hands, *
    and make firm the feeble knees.
Say to the anxious, "Be strong, do not fear! *
    Here is your God, coming with judgment
        to save you."

**Scripture**    "Lord, when was it that we saw you hungry and gave you food, or thirsty and gave you something to drink? And when was it that we saw you a stranger and welcomed you, or naked and gave you clothing? And when was it that we saw you sick or in prison and visited you?" And the king will answer them, "Truly I tell you, just as you did it to one of the least of these who are members of my family, you did it to me."    Matthew 25:37-40

**Meditation**  Do you wish to honor the body of the Saviour? Do not despise it when it is naked. Do not honor it in church with silk vestments, while outside you are leaving it numb with cold and naked. He who said, "This is my body," and made it so by his word, is the same that said, "You saw me hungry and you gave me no food. As you did it not to the least of these, you did it not to me." Honor him then by sharing your property with the poor, for what God needs is not golden chalices, but golden souls.

John Chrysostom [75]

*Who are the hungry and naked in our daily world, and how will we relieve their suffering?*

**Prayers**    God of hope, help us who struggle in our daily work.
When we lose our purpose,
**renew our hope in you.**
When we bow to hatred,
**renew our trust in you.**
When we despair of bliss,
**renew our joy in you.**
When we take offense at others,
**renew our life in you.**
When we compromise our values,
**renew our faith in you.**
When we cherish regrets,
**renew our freedom in you.**
When we surrender to despair,
**renew our hope in you.**
As we accept your renewing love, we offer our prayers
to you:

*Here, the people may add particular intercessions
or thanksgivings.*

Hold us, and all people, in your loving care,
**and may we be hope for others.**

**Lord's Prayer**

**Prayer**    God of hope, from you come every blessing and all
peace: Show us that, in the midst of our struggles,
you are with us. Give us the abundance of your
grace that we may do the work you give us to do
and that we may be for the world a sign of your
presence; through Christ, the Way and the Truth.
**Amen.**

**Going Out**    Renew and strengthen us, eternal God,
**as we prepare for resurrection.**

71

# Love

*As shadows lengthen, we are filled by the day's encounters; now, more than ever, we accept the depth and breadth of God's grace.*

**Opening**    May our sacrifice be love
**as we practice mercy on earth.**

**Prayer**    God of love, the day is long and its burden is heavy:
Give us grace to see your hand at work in the
lives of those around us so that adversity will not
overwhelm us, nor resentments possess us. Remain
with us, for the sake of Jesus Christ, our Saviour.
**Amen.**

**Praise**    *Love Bade Me Welcome*
Love bade me welcome; yet my soul drew back,
Guilty of dust and sin.
But quick-eye'd Love, observing me grow slack
From my first entrance in,
Drew nearer to me, sweetly questioning
If I lack'd anything.
A guest, I answer'd, worthy to be here:
Love said, You shall be he.
I, the unkind, ungrateful? Ah, my dear,
I cannot look on Thee.
Love took my hand and smiling did reply,
Who made the eyes, but I?
Truth, Lord, but I have marred them: let my shame
Go where it doth deserve.
And know you not, says Love, Who bore the blame?
My dear, then I will serve.
You must sit down, says Love, and taste my meat.
So I did sit and eat.
                        George Herbert [76]

| Scripture | Beloved, let us love one another, because love is from God; everyone who loves is born of God and knows God. |
|---|---|

I John 4:7

| Meditation | We cannot know whether we love God although there may be strong reason for thinking so, but there can be no doubt about whether we love our neighbour or not. Be sure that, in proportion as you advance in affection for sisters and brothers, you are increasing your love of God. |
|---|---|

Teresa of Avila [77]

*Who is hard to love just now? What would it cost us to love that one?*

| Prayers | O God, you beckon us with promises of love;<br>**Fulfill our desire for you.**<br>You pursue us even when we flee from you;<br>**Bring us to our right minds.**<br>You delight in us and show us your compassion;<br>**Make us mindful of the deep need in the world.** |
|---|---|

*Here, the people may add particular intercessions or thanksgivings.*

You give us the gift of your unbounded love;
**Pour out your love on all the world.**

### Lord's Prayer

| Prayer | Merciful God, return us now to working and relating in our world; return us, stimulated by hope, strengthened by faith, and directed by love. Thus, we are heartened to reconcile all people, created, redeemed, and sustained by you. In the name of Christ. **Amen.** [78] |
|---|---|

| Going Out | May our sacrifice be love<br>**as we practice mercy on earth.** |
|---|---|

# Forgiveness

*Vespers*      (Traditional hour: evening/end of the day)

*As we turn on lamps at dusk, we greet the evening by welcoming God to abide with us anew.*

**Opening**      Wherever we stray,
**lead us back to the rock of your love.**

**Prayer**      Holy God, in love you created us and called our being "good." With open hearts, we praise you for your unfailing love. With open hands, we offer you our labours. Bless and guide us now as our day turns toward evening; through your grace, may we share with others the love we receive from you. In the name of God our Creator, Jesus our brother, and the Spirit who lights our way. **Amen.**

**Song of praise**

*A Song of Christ's Goodness* [79]

Jesus, as a mother you gather your people to you; *
you are gentle with us as a mother with her children.
Often you weep over our sins and our pride, *
    tenderly you draw us from hatred and judgment.
You comfort us in sorrow and bind up our wounds, *
    in sickness you nurse us and with pure milk you
        feed us.
Jesus, by your dying, we are born to new life; *
    by your anguish and labour we come forth in
    joy.
Despair turns to hope through your sweet goodness; *
    through your gentleness, we find comfort in fear.
Your warmth gives life to the dead, *
    your touch makes sinners righteous.
Lord Jesus, in your mercy, heal us; *
    in your love and tenderness, remake us.
May your love prepare us for the beauty of heaven.

Anselm of Canterbury

74

**Scripture**   Listen to me, you that pursue righteousness, you that seek the Lord. Look to the rock from which you were hewn, and to the quarry from which you were dug. For the Lord will comfort Zion; he will comfort all her waste places, and will make her wilderness like Eden, her desert like the garden of the Lord; joy and gladness will be found in her, thanksgiving and the voice of song.

Isaiah 51:1, 3

**Meditation**   This only do I ask of your extreme kindness. That you convert me wholly to you and you allow nothing to prevent me from wending my way to you.

Saint Augustine

*What will we set aside now that blocks our way to God?*

**Confession**   **Lord Jesus, you come into our lives**
**when we are least prepared for you.**
**As you enfolded your betrayers,**
**so embrace us who struggle to love.**
**Reconcile us with our sisters and brothers,**
**and, for the sake of your love,**
**forgive us all our sins.**

**Assurance of Pardon**   Psalm 103:11-13 [80]

As far as the heavens are high above the earth,
so great is your loving response to those who are
   humble;
so far does your enduring strength
uphold those who face the darkness within.
As parents are concerned for their children,
so you come to those who reach out in faith.

**Prayers**      For all we have accomplished this day,
          **we bless God's name.**
          For now, when we turn from labour to home,
          **we bless God's name.**
          For those tasks we left undone this day,
          **we invite God's love.**
          For those wounds we gave or received this day,
          **we invite God's love.**
          For our hopes and concerns for tomorrow,
          **we invite God's love.**
          For the gift of our presence this hour,
          **we seek God's grace.**
          For trust that God's love is all we need,
          **we seek God's grace.**

          *Here, the people may add particular intercessions
          or thanksgivings.*

          For these praises and preoccupations of our hearts,
          **we find our hope in God.**

**Lord's Prayer**

**Prayer**      Holy One, we bless your name and thank you for
          the gift of this day:
          May the Light of the world guide us, the Life of the
          world refresh us, and the Hope of the world be our
          companion, that we may be the reconciling power
          of Christ in the world. We ask this for your mercy's
          sake. **Amen.**

**Going Out**   Wherever we stray,
          **lead us back to the rock of your love.**

# Trust

*Compline*   (Traditional hour: night/bedtime)

*We sum up this day with a bedtime prayer to examine our conscience and offer our actions to God.*

**Opening**       Give us the grace to rely on you:
**may we always trust in your goodness.**

**Prayer**        Enduring presence, goal and guide, you go before
and await our coming. Only our thirst compels us
beyond complaint to conversation, beyond rejection
to relation. Pour your love into our hearts that,
refreshed and renewed, we may invite others to the
living water given to us in Jesus Christ our Lord.
**Amen.** [81]

**Praise**        *O God of gentle strength*

O God of gentle strength, your love embraces me.
Within the sureness of your care my heart rests
    willingly.

Your waters of rebirth have claimed us as your
    own.
As members of one body, we shall never be alone.

And when life's challenges eclipse our minds with
    doubt,
let holy wisdom spark a flame to drive the darkness
    out.

Where will the journey lead? The path may be
    obscure.
But promised hope of things unseen will keep our
    footing sure.

Words: Patricia B. Clark (b. 1938) [82]

**Scripture**   Thus says the Lord God, the Holy One of Israel: In returning and rest you shall be saved; in quietness and confidence shall be your strength. Therefore the Lord waits to be gracious to you; therefore he will rise up to show mercy to you. For the Lord is a God of justice; blessed are all those who wait for the Lord.                                      Isaiah 30:15a, 18

**Meditation**  The birds have vanished into the sky,
and now the last cloud drains away.

We sit together, the mountain and me,
until only the mountain remains.
                                                                    Li Po, 8th-century poet [83]

*What do we need to trust this fully in God's grace?*

**Prayer**      Patient and compassionate God,
We so want to trust in your love.
**Hear our longing.**
We hope for healing in our lives and the lives
        of others:

*Here, the people may add particular intercessions
or thanksgivings.*

Hear our prayers.
**Heed our holy desires.**
We confess our impatience and anxiety.
**We seek your grace.**

**The Lord's Prayer**

**Prayer**     O Lord and Ruler of our life: Deliver us from the spirit of sloth, idle talk, faint-heartedness, and lust for power; and grant unto us, your servants, a spirit of integrity, humility, patience and love. Sovereign God, grant us the ability to see our own faults and not to judge another's; for you are blessed to the ages of ages. **Amen.** [84]

**Closing**    Give us the grace to rely on you:
**may we always trust in your goodness.**

# Watch

*Vigils*        (Traditional hour: late night)

*Like nuns and monks at prayer, we can listen in the stillness of the night to hear God's call.*

**Opening**     Be present with me, Holy One,
                **as I watch with you.**

**Scripture**   O my strength, I will watch for you; for you,
                O God, are my stronghold.                    Psalm 59:9

**Meditation** *Where do I need God's strength?*

**Prayer**      Keep watch, dear Lord, with those who work, or
                watch, or weep this night, and give your angels
                charge over those who sleep. Tend the sick, Lord
                Christ; give rest to the weary, bless the dying,
                soothe the suffering, pity the afflicted, shield the
                joyous; and all for your love's sake. **Amen.** [85]

**Closing**     Be present with me, Holy One,
                **as I watch with you.**

# Holy Week

The theme of Holy Week is Jesus' passion: his suffering and death on the cross. The rites of Holy Week are at the very heart of the Christian year, indeed of our Christian faith. And for many of us they are, year after year, the most meaningful and life-changing services of the church.

It is vital to keep a broad perspective during this week. We walk through the days of Jesus' suffering and death because we believe they had a purpose — the salvation of the world. We believe Jesus' death conquered death itself for us all: that is the only reason why the Friday on which he died can be called "good." Even while we are sobered by the solemn reading of the gospel stories describing Jesus' death and deeply saddened by the ongoing violence in our world, from that day in Jerusalem to this Good Friday, we hold on to the faith that in Jesus God has brought about a new creation, and death itself has been conquered. "We have been buried with him by baptism into death," wrote the apostle Paul soon after Jesus' death, "so that, just as Christ was raised from the dead by the glory of the Father, so we too might walk in newness of life" (Romans 6:4).

# Praise

*Lauds*        (Traditional hour: dawn/waking up)

Laudate, omnes gentes, laudate Dominum!
[*Sing praises, all people, sing praises to the Lord!*]
*We greet the new day by praising the Creator*
*(the ancient name for this hour, Lauds, means "praise").*

**Opening**     Come darkness or light
              **I call on your name, holy Lord.**

**Scripture**   I love you, O God, because you have heard the
              voice of my supplication.                    Psalm 116:1a

**Meditation** *What do I offer God at this hour?*

**Prayer**      O Holy One, whatever comes this day, let me seek
              you with confidence and trust. **Amen.**

**Going Out** Come darkness or light,
              **I call on your name, holy Lord.**

# Discernment

*Prime*        (Traditional hour: morning/start of the day)

*As we begin the day, we focus on our calling to live faithfully,*
*for who knows what today holds?*

**Opening**     You have called us in righteousness.
               **Let us respond with justice.**

**Prayer**      God of steadfast love, light of the blind and
               liberator of the oppressed, we see your holy purpose
               in the tender compassion of Jesus, who calls us
               into new and living friendship with you: May we
               who take shelter in the shadow of your wings be
               filled with the grace of his tender caring; may we
               who stumble in selfish darkness see your glory in
               the light of his self-giving; we ask this through
               him whose suffering is victorious, Jesus Christ our
               Saviour. **Amen.** [86]

**Song of praise**
               *You Laid Aside Your Rightful Reputation*

               You laid aside your rightful reputation
               and gave no heed to what the world might say;
               served as a slave and laid aside your garments
               to wash the feet of those who walked your way.

               You touched the leper, ate with those rejected,
               received the worship of a woman's tears:
               You shed the pride that keeps us from the freedom
               to love our neighbour, laying down our fears.

               Help us to follow, Jesus, where you lead us
               to love, to serve, our own lives laying down;
               to walk your way of humble, costly service,
               a cross its end, a ring of thorns its crown.

Draw us to love you and with your love
   transform us:
the love we've seen, the love we've touched and
   known;
enlarge our hearts and with compassion fill us
to love, to serve, to follow you alone.

Words: Rosalind Brown (b. 1953) [87]

**Scripture**    Here is my servant, whom I uphold, my chosen,
   in whom my soul delights;
I have put my spirit upon him; he will bring forth
   justice to the nations.
He will not cry or lift up his voice, or make it heard
   in the street;
a bruised reed he will not break, and a dimly
   burning wick he will not quench;
he will faithfully bring forth justice.        Isaiah 42:1-4

**Meditation**  We must get ready then. Our journey requires a
rejuvenated faith. We must set high standards. We
must rely on the gospel to guide us. It will help us
to follow Christ and grow better acquainted with
him so we are prepared to live with Jesus in his
heavenly kingdom.        from *The Rule of St. Benedict*

*Where does our faith need rejuvenation today?*
*How will we let the gospel guide us?*

**Affirmation**  As children of God, we affirm:
That God, who is Love, created all and called it
   good,
that God is present with all of creation, and that,
in darkness and in light, God is faithful;
therefore we, too, seek to be faithful.

That Jesus came to show us Love with a human
    face,
that he taught justice and reconciliation and
    suffered on our behalf,
and that through his faithful example, he embodies
    hope;
therefore we, too, seek to be people of justice,
    reconciliation, and hope.

That the Holy Spirit guides and accompanies us,
that this same Spirit offers wisdom and
    discernment,
and that, when we are open, the Spirit can always
    find a way;
therefore, we seek to be people filled with God's
    Spirit:
discerning, loving and transforming our world.
Amen.

**Prayers**    Jesus, faithful servant of God,
sometimes it is difficult for us to know how
    to be faithful:
**Help us discern your will and follow you with**
    **gladness.**
Jesus, faithful servant of God,
in this most holy of weeks, we see the
    brokenness of our world:
**Help us be people who faithfully bring forth justice.**
Jesus, faithful servant of God,
we know the world longs for healing:
**Help us be people of hope and bearers of light.**
Jesus, faithful servant of God,
we want to be the people you long for us to be:
**Help us walk in your way of love.**

*Here, the people may add particular intercessions
or thanksgivings.*

**Lord's Prayer**

**Prayer**    Loving God, as we seek to know and follow you more faithfully, we pray you will open and fill our hearts with the love and knowledge of your Son, Jesus. May we see ever more clearly what it is you call us to, and may we respond with lives of joy and justice. **Amen.**

**Going Out**  You have called us in righteousness.
**Let us respond with justice.**

# Wisdom

*Terce*          (Traditional hour: mid-morning)

*Having asked for direction and guidance, we pray now to equip ourselves properly for the journey ahead.*

**Opening**      Teach us to seek your wisdom
                 **as we embrace the folly of your love.**

**Prayer**       Holy and immortal God, from earliest times you
                 have named us and called us into Discipleship:
                 Teach us to follow the One whose light scatters
                 the darkness of our world, that we may walk as
                 children of the light. **Amen.** [88]

**Praise**       *Faithful Cross, Above All Other*
                 *(Crux fidelis inter omnes)*

                 Faithful cross, above all other:
                 one and only noble tree!
                 None in foliage, none in blossom,
                 none in fruit thy peer may be:
                 sweetest wood and sweetest iron,
                 sweetest weight is hung on thee.

                 Bend thy boughs, O tree of glory!
                 Thy relaxing sinews bend;
                 for awhile the ancient rigor
                 that thy birth bestowed, suspend;
                 and the King of heavenly beauty
                 gently on thy arms extend.

                 Words: Venantius Honorius Fortunatus (540-600?);<br>trans. after John Mason Neale (1818-1866)

**Scripture**    For the message about the cross is foolishness to
                 those who are perishing, but to us who are being
                 saved, it is the power of God. For it is written,
                 "I will destroy the wisdom of the wise, and the

discernment of the discerning I will thwart. For
God's foolishness is wiser than human wisdom, and
God's weakness is stronger than human strength.

1 Corinthians 1: 18-19, 25

**Meditation** To make of his story something that could neither
startle, nor shock, nor terrify, nor excite, nor inspire
a living soul is to crucify the Son of God afresh.

Dorothy L. Sayers (1893-1957) [89]

*Where do we seek courage and wisdom to proclaim
the gospel in its fullness?*

**Prayers**  God of mercy,
**Make us wise with your foolish love.**
God of salvation,
**Open our eyes again to see the power of your grace.**
God of all who seek to follow,
**Guide us in your faithful way.**

*Here, the people may add particular intercessions
or thanksgivings.*

**Lord's Prayer**

**Prayer**  Christ our Lord, you refused the way of domination
and died the death of a slave:
May we also refuse to lord it over those who are
subject to us, but share the weight of authority so
that all may be empowered; in your name. **Amen.** [90]

**Going Out** Teach us to seek your wisdom.
**as we embrace the folly of your love.**

# Perseverance and Renewal

*Sext*        (Traditional hour: mid-day)

*As we pause to feed our bodies in the middle of the day, we pause also to feed our souls by vowing again to live faithfully.*

**Opening**     Be pleased, O God, to deliver us.
            **Make haste, Holy One, to help us.**  (Psalm 70:1)

**Prayer**      Blessed Saviour, at this hour you hung upon the
            cross, stretching out your loving arms:
            Grant that all the peoples of the earth may look to
            you and be saved; for your tender mercies' sake.
            **Amen.** [91]

**Praise**      *Take My Hand, Precious Lord*

            Precious Lord, take my hand,
            lead me on, let me stand,
            I am tired, I am weak, I am worn;
            through the storm, through the night,
            lead me on to the light,
            take my hand, precious Lord,
            lead me on.

            When my way grows drear,
            precious Lord, linger near,
            when my life is almost gone;
            hear my cry, hear my call,
            hold my hand, lest I fall,
            take my hand, precious Lord,
            lead me on.

When the darkness appears
and the night draws near,
and the day is past and gone;
at the river I stand,
guide my feet, hold my hand,
take my hand, precious Lord,
lead me on.

Words: Thomas A. Dorsey (1899-1993)

**Scripture** For I [Paul] received from the Lord what I also
handed on to you, that the Lord Jesus, on the
night when he was betrayed, took a loaf of bread,
and when he had given thanks, he broke it and
said, "This is my body that is for you. Do this in
remembrance of me." In the same way he took
the cup also, after supper, saying, "This cup is the
new covenant in my blood. Do this, as often as you
drink it, in remembrance of me." For as often as
you eat this bread and drink the cup, you proclaim
the Lord's death until he comes.     1 Corinthians 11:23-26

**Meditation** The soul must live in hope.

Beatrijs of Nazareth (1200-1268), *Seven Manners of Living*

*Where do we need nourishment and hope this
hour? This week?*

**Prayers** Precious Lord, you know what it means to carry
a heavy load:
**Help us entrust our burdens to you.**
Holy Lord, you walked many a winding road:
**Help us see all parts of our lives as sacred.**
Gracious Lord, so many hunger and thirst in
our world:
**Strengthen us for service, so we may be bread and
wine for others.**
Precious Lord, as we return to the work of this day:
**Take our hands and lead us on.**

*Here, the people may add particular intercessions
or thanksgivings.*

**Lord's Prayer**

Prayer       Eternal God, in the sharing of a meal, your Son
             established a new covenant for all people, and in
             the washing of feet he showed us the dignity of
             service: Grant that by the power of the Holy Spirit
             these signs of our life in faith may speak again in
             our hearts, feed our spirits, and refresh our bodies.
             **Amen.** [92]

Going Out    Be pleased, O God, to deliver us.
             **Make haste, Holy One, to help us.**

                                                      Psalm 70:1

# Love

*None*     (Traditional hour: afternoon)

*As shadows lengthen, we are filled by the day's encounters; now, more than ever, we accept the depth and breadth of God's grace.*

**Opening**     You lavish love upon us.
          **Make us people of extravagant love.**

**Prayer**     Holy God, lover of our souls, we come before you
          as people created by and for love:
          Gather us in this time to hear again your word of
          love, to renew our trust in its breadth and depth.
          In the sacrifice of your love for us, may we find
          renewal and be your love in the world. **Amen.**

**Praise**     *My Song Is Love Unknown*

          My song is love unknown, my Saviour's love to me,
          love to the loveless shown that they might lovely be.
          O who am I that for my sake my Lord
          should take frail flesh, and die?

          He came from his blest throne salvation to bestow,
          but men made strange, and none the longed for
              Christ would know.
          But O my friend, my friend indeed,
          who at my need his life did spend.

          Sometimes they strew his way, and his strong
              praises sing,
          resounding all the day hosannas to their King.
          then "Crucify!" is all their breath,
          and for his death they thirst and cry.

Why, what hath my Lord done? What makes this
      rage and spite?
He made the lame to run, he gave the blind their sight.
Sweet injuries! Yet they at these themselves displease,
and 'gainst him rise.

Here might I stay and sing, no story so divine;
never was love, dear Christ, never was grief like thine.
this is my friend, in whose sweet praise
I all my days could gladly spend.

Words (alt): Samuel Crossman (1624-1683)

**Scripture**    Six days before the Passover, Jesus came to Bethany,
the home of Lazarus, whom he had raised from the
dead. Martha served, and Lazarus was one of those
at table with him. Mary took a pound of costly
perfume made with pure nard, anointed Jesus' feet,
and wiped them with her hair. The house was filled
with the fragrance of the perfume.          John 12:1-3

**Meditation** Look
what happens to the scale
when love
holds
it.
It
stops
working.                              Kafir (c.1440-1518) [93]

*Where might we "waste" love this week?*

93

| | |
|---|---|
| Prayers | Jesus, Holy One of God,<br>**You embodied love for us.**<br>Jesus, Holy One of God,<br>**You accepted love from all who offered.**<br>Jesus, Holy One of God,<br>**We acknowledge our need for your love.**<br><br>Teach us, we pray:<br>**The courage to both give and receive love,**<br>**the humility to admit when we have not**<br>    **loved well, and**<br>**the faith to trust that your love is enough.**<br><br>*Here, the people may add particular intercessions*<br>*or thanksgivings.* |

**Lord's Prayer**

| | |
|---|---|
| Prayer | Holy Spirit, fill us with godly love.<br>Free us from all that resists loving and being loved.<br>Empower us to love as Jesus did.<br>In his gracious name we pray. **Amen.** |
| Going Out | You lavish love upon us.<br>**Make us people of extravagant love.** |

# Forgiveness

*Vespers*     (Traditional hour: evening/end of day)

*As we turn on lamps at dusk, we greet the evening by welcoming God to abide with us anew.*

**Opening**     In the fullness of our humanity,
              **heal us, gracious Saviour.**

**Prayer**      Troubled God, in every generation you call your
              people to contend against the brutality of sin and
              betrayal: Keep us steadfast even in our fear and
              uncertainty, so that we may follow where Jesus has
              led the way. **Amen.** [94]

**Praise**      *As in That Upper Room, You Left Your Seat*

              As in that upper room you left your seat
              and took a towel and chose a servant's part,
              so for today, Lord, wash again my feet,
              who in your mercy died to cleanse my heart.

              I bow before you, all my sin confessed,
              to hear again the words of love you said;
              and at your table, as your honored guest,
              I take and eat the true and living bread.

              So in remembrance of your life laid down
              I come to praise you for your grace divine;
              saved by your cross, and subject to your reign,
              strengthened for service by the bread and wine.
                        Words (alt): Timothy Dudley-Smith (b. 1926) [95]

**Scripture**  At that moment, while Peter was still speaking, the cock crowed. The Lord turned and looked at Peter. Then Peter remembered the word of the Lord, how he had said to him, "Before the cock crows today, you will deny me three times." And Peter went out and wept bitterly.

Luke 22: 60b-62

**Meditation**  [God says]: "No matter what you have done, I love you for your own sake. Come to me with your misery and your sins, with your trouble and your needs, and with all your longing to be loved. I stand at the door of your heart and knock. Open to me, for I thirst for you."

Mother Teresa (1910-1997) [96]

*Where do we long to be loved and forgiven at this hour?*

**Confession**  **We are human: we strive to love, but we often fail. Jesus, we confess that we do not always answer** when you call us to bear your light in the world. Although we long for love, too often we fail
    to accept it or to offer it.
Help us let go of our failings.
Renew our hearts.
**Fill us anew with your love.  Amen.**

**Assurance of Pardon**
    God says to us, "I love you for your own sake."
    Know that you are loved and forgiven.
    Jesus invites us to pick up our lives anew
    And walk in love.

**Prayers**       God of extravagant love,
**Transform us with the freedom of forgiveness.**
God of unbounded, sacrificial love,
**Teach us to give ourselves in joyful service.**
God whose love persists even in the darkest hour,
**Deepen our faith, renew our spirits and strengthen
    our confidence in you,**
**that we may truly learn to walk in self-giving love.**

*Here, the people may add particular intercessions
or thanksgivings.*

**Lord's Prayer**

**Prayer**       Christ our victim, whose beauty was disfigured
upon the cross: Open wide your arms to embrace
our tortured world, that we may not turn away our
eyes, but abandon ourselves to your mercy.
**Amen.** [97]

**Going Out**  In the fullness of our humanity,
**heal us, gracious Saviour.**

# Trust

*Compline*   (Traditional hour: night/bedtime)

*We sum up this day with a bedtime prayer to examine our conscience and offer our actions to God.*

**Opening**   Into your hands we entrust our souls,
**for you have redeemed us, O God of truth.**

**Prayer**   Christ our God, your love is poured out in death for our sakes: Hold us in your embrace as we wait for Easter's dawn. Comfort us with the promise that no power on earth, not even death itself, can separate us from your love; and strengthen us to wait until you are revealed to us in all your risen glory. **Amen.** 98

**Praise**   *I Want Jesus to Walk with Me*

I want Jesus to walk with me;
I want Jesus to walk with me
All along my pilgrim journey.
Lord, I want Jesus to walk with me.

In my trials, Lord walk with me;
In my trials, Lord walk with me;
When the shades of life are falling,
Lord, I want Jesus to walk with me.

In my sorrows, Lord walk with me;
In my sorrows, Lord walk with me;
When my heart within is aching,
Lord, I want Jesus to walk with me.

Text: traditional

**Scripture**    Then Jesus, crying with a loud voice, said, "Father, into your hands I commend my spirit."    Luke 23:46a

**Meditation**    Little by little, God grows us ever more in grace because God wants to be seen and sought. God wants to be awaited and trusted.
                    Julian of Norwich (1342-1420), *Revelations*

*Jesus entrusted his soul to God's care. What should we entrust to God this hour?*

**Prayers**    Holy God, friend of the friendless,
    **Deepen our trust in your faithfulness.**
    Jesus, our brother, loving even unto death,
    **Walk with us as we grow in trust and love.**
    Holy Spirit, source of all life,
    **Give us eyes that see your glory
    and hearts that long for your grace.**

*Here, the people may add particular intercessions or thanksgivings.*

## Lord's Prayer

**Prayer**    Eternal God, rock and refuge, with roots grown old in the earth, riverbeds run dry, and flowers withered in the field, we wait for revival and release: Abide with us until we come alive in the sunrise of your glory. **Amen.** [99]

**Closing**    Into your hands we entrust our souls,
    **for you have redeemed us, O God of truth.**

# Watch

*Vigils* (Traditional hour: late night)

*Like nuns and monks at prayer, we can listen in the stillness of the night to hear God's call.*

**Opening**  Lord Jesus, as I watch and pray,
**remain here with me.**

**Scripture**  Jesus said to them, "I am deeply grieved, even to death; remain here, and keep awake." Mark 14:34

**Meditation**  *What will I watch and pray about this hour?*

**Prayers**  Jesus, alongside your suffering, you also bear my wounds. I offer you all the grief and worries I carry at this hour: may they be transformed by your love. **Amen.**

**Closing**  Lord Jesus, as I watch and pray,
**remain here with me.**

# Easter

Easter, the oldest celebration of the Christian year, is not a single day but an entire season: Easter lasts fifty days, from Easter Day (the Sunday of the Resurrection) through the Day of Pentecost. The season also includes the feast of the Ascension, when the resurrected Jesus ascended to heaven and was seen on earth no longer. Throughout the year every Sunday — even during Lent — is considered a little Easter, a mini feast of the resurrection on what Christians have called the first day of the week. The primary theme of Easter is the resurrection: on this day Jesus was raised from the dead, overcoming the power of death and the grave. We celebrate that we, too, are raised to everlasting life with him in our baptism.

At Pentecost we celebrate the outpouring of the Holy Spirit and the ongoing life of the Holy Spirit in the church today. It is the Holy Spirit who breathes life into the Body of Christ, the church; it is the Holy Spirit who provides the gifts and guidance needed to sustain our life. At every Eucharist we pray that the Holy Spirit will sanctify the bread and wine of communion to be "the Body and Blood of your Son, the holy food and drink of new and unending life in him." We also pray that the Spirit will "sanctify us also" so that we may receive the Eucharist with faith and serve God "in unity, constancy, and peace." It is the Holy Spirit who makes God present and alive in our hearts.

# Praise

*Lauds* (Traditional hour: dawn/waking up)

*Laudate, omnes gentes, laudate Dominum!*
*[Sing praises, all people, sing praises to the Lord!]*
*We greet the new day by praising the Creator*
*(the ancient name for this hour, Lauds, means "praise").*

**Opening** Alleluia! Christ is risen!
**Christ is risen indeed! Alleluia!**

**Scripture** If anyone is in Christ, there is a new creation:
everything old has passed away;
see, everything has become new! 2 Corinthians 5:17

**Meditation** *Today, how will I live joyfully in God's new*
*creation?*

**Prayer** As the morning approaches, I pray:
Risen Lord, be my light, my life, and my hope.
Come: enlighten my darkness and bring me life
by your life. **Amen.**

**Going Out** Alleluia! Christ is risen!
**Christ is risen indeed! Alleluia!**

# Discernment

*Prime*     (Traditional hour: morning/start of the day)

*As we begin the day, we focus on our calling to live faithfully, for who knows what today holds?*

**Opening**     Alleluia! O God, may the empty tomb
**fill our hearts with faith. Alleluia!**

**Prayer**     Jesus, our way, our truth, and our life: As the gift of this new day unfolds, open our hearts and minds to you, that we may see you clearly and follow where you lead; to you, risen Saviour, we offer praise, now and always. **Amen.**

**Praise**     *A Song of Our Adoption*  (Ephesians 1:3-10) [100]

Blessed are you, the God and Father of our
        Lord Jesus Christ, *
    for you have blessed us in Christ
    with every spiritual blessing in the heavenly places.
Before the world was made, you chose us to be
        yours in Christ, *
    that we should be holy and blameless before you.
You destined us for adoption as your children
        through Jesus Christ, *
    according to the good pleasure of your will,
To the praise of your glorious grace, *
    that you have freely given us in the Beloved.
In you, we have redemption through the blood
        of Christ, *
    the forgiveness of our sins,
According to the riches of your grace*
    which you have lavished upon us.
You have made known to us, in all wisdom
        and insight,*
    the mystery of your will,

According to your good pleasure which you set
        forth in Christ,*
    as a plan for the fullness of time,
To gather together all things in Christ,*
    things in heaven and things on earth.

Scripture  The angel said to the women at the tomb, "I know
that you are looking for Jesus, who was crucified.
He is not here, for he has been raised, as he said."

Matthew 28:6

Meditation  *The Trouble with Easter*
But ... I want the tomb full, like temple or tent —
with the Holy enshrouded in fabric un-rent.
Yes, I want death preserved in sweet-smelling spice;
not my neighbour perspiring the aroma of Christ.

Julia McCray-Goldsmith

*How will we together embrace the gift of life in all
its fullness today?*

Affirmation
Christ Jesus, though in the form of God,
    did not exploit equality with God
    but emptied himself,
    in the form of a slave,
    born in human likeness.
And being found in human form,
    he humbled himself
    and became obedient to the point of death —
    even death on a cross.
Therefore, God also highly exalted him
    and gave him the name
    that is above every name,
so that at the name of Jesus
    every knee should bend,
    in heaven and on earth and under the earth,

and every tongue should confess
that Jesus Christ is Lord,
to the glory of God the Father.

Philippians 2:5-11

Prayers   In the work we do this day,
**May the risen Christ teach us.**
In the challenges we face this day,
**May the risen Christ guide us.**
Through the people we meet this day,
**May the risen Christ renew us.**

*Here, the people may add particular intercessions
or thanksgivings.*

As we respond to the hungers and hurts of this
world,
**May the Spirit of the risen Christ strengthen us.**

## Lord's Prayer

Prayer   Jesus, our friend and saviour: Guide us in this new
day, that we may know God's desire for us and gain
strength and courage to live as beloved children of
God. **Amen.**

Going Out   Alleluia! O God, may the empty tomb
**fill our hearts with faith. Alleluia!**

# Wisdom

*Terce*        (Traditional hour: mid-morning)

*Having asked for direction and guidance, we pray now to equip ourselves properly for the journey ahead.*

**Opening**     Alleluia! Risen Lord, come be with us,
              **and teach our hearts to live in you. Alleluia!**

**Prayer**      Jesus, divine companion: As the day unfolds, give us
              strength to understand and eyes to see, as you teach
              us to walk the soft earth, related to all that lives.
              **Amen.** [101]

**Praise**      *A Song of Wisdom* (Wisdom 10:15-19, 20b-21) [102]

              Wisdom freed from a nation of oppressors *
                  a holy people and a blameless race.
              She entered the soul of a servant of the Lord, *
                  withstood dread rulers with wonders and signs.

              To the saints she gave the reward of their labours, *
                  and led them by a marvelous way;
              She was their shelter by day *
                  and a blaze of stars by night.

              She brought them across the Red Sea, *
                  she led them through mighty waters;
              But their enemies she swallowed in the waves *
                  and spewed them out from the depths of the abyss.

              And then, Lord, the righteous sang hymns to
                      your Name *
                  and praised with one voice your protecting hand;
              For Wisdom opened the mouths of the mute *
                  and gave speech to the tongues of a new-born
                      people.

**Scripture**   We have been buried with Christ by baptism into death, so that, just as Christ was raised from the dead by the glory of the Father, so we too might walk in newness of life.                                     Romans 6:4

**Meditation** I asked my Lord, and he listened to me.
                                                                 St. Scholastica (d. 543)

*Where do we ask for God's wisdom today?*

**Prayers**    Risen Christ, open our hearts to your grace
                     and truth.
               **May we walk in newness of life.**
               Teach us to love others in the power of the Spirit.
               **May we walk in newness of life.**

               *Here, the people may add particular intercessions
               or thanksgivings.*

               Strengthen us as witnesses to your love.
               **May we walk in newness of life.**

**Lord's Prayer**

**Prayer**     God our Deliverer, by water and the Holy Spirit
               we have been buried with Christ and raised to the
               new life of grace: Give us inquiring and discerning
               hearts, the courage to will and to persevere, a spirit
               to know and to love you, and the gift of joy and
               wonder in all your works. **Amen.**

**Going Out**  Alleluia! Risen Lord, come be with us,
               **and teach our hearts to live in you. Alleluia!**

# Perseverance and Renewal

*Sext*        (Traditional hour: mid-day)

*As we pause to feed our bodies in the middle of the day, we pause also to feed our souls by vowing again to live faithfully.*

**Opening**    Alleluia! Risen Lord,
              **deepen our desire for you. Alleluia!**

**Prayer**     God of steadfast love: Turn our hearts to you, that
              we may once again delight in your goodness and
              rejoice in the good news of the risen Christ; in
              whose name we pray. **Amen.**

**Praise**     *Psalm 118:19-24*

              Open for me the gates of righteousness;
                  I will enter them; I will offer thanks to the Lord.
              "This is the gate of the Lord;
                  the righteous shall enter through it."
              I will give thanks to you, for you answered me
                  and have become my salvation.
              The same stone that the builders rejected
                  has become the chief cornerstone.
              This is the Lord's doing,
                  and it is marvelous in our eyes.
              On this day that the Lord has acted,
                  we will rejoice and be glad in it.

**Scripture**  Mary Magdalene, and Mary the mother of James,
              and Salome bought spices, so that they might go
              and anoint Jesus. ...They had been saying to one
              another, "Who will roll away the stone for us from
              the entrance to the tomb?" When they looked up,
              they saw that the stone, which was very large, had
              already been rolled back.          Mark 16:1, 3-4

**Meditation**  It is my deepest belief that only by giving our lives do we find life.  Cesar Chavez [103]

*What enables us to give our lives for others?*

**Prayers**  Lord Jesus, you rise triumphant over death and the grave:
**Christ our life, save us.**
Christ, the Lord of life, raise us to new life:
**Christ our life, save us.**

*Here, the people may add particular intercessions or thanksgivings.*

In a world where so many suffer because of hunger and injustice:
**Christ our life, save us.**

**Lord's Prayer**

**Prayer**  Living God, long ago, faithful women proclaimed the good news of Jesus' resurrection, and the world was changed forever: Teach us to keep faith with them, that our witness may be as bold, our love as deep, and our faith as true. **Amen.** [104]

**Going Out**  Alleluia! Risen Lord,
**deepen our desire for you. Alleluia!**

# Love

*As shadows lengthen, we are filled by the day's encounters; now, more than ever, we accept the depth and breadth of God's grace.*

**Opening**      Alleluia! Come to us, O risen Lord,
              **and enliven us with your eternal love. Alleluia!**

**Prayer**      Loving God, we no longer look for Jesus among the
              dead, for he is alive in our world, our church and
              our hearts. Renew and strengthen us in the risen life
              we share in Christ, in whose name we pray. **Amen.**

**Praise**      *A Song of Faith*   (1 Peter 1:3-4,18-21) [105]

              Blessed be the God and Father of our Lord
                  Jesus Christ, *
                by divine mercy we have a new birth into a
                  living hope;
              Through the resurrection of Jesus Christ from
                  the dead, *
                we have an inheritance that is imperishable in
                  heaven.
              The ransom that was paid to free us *
                was not paid in silver or gold
              But in the precious blood of Christ, *
                the Lamb without spot or stain.
              God raised Jesus from the dead and gave him glory *
                so that we might have faith and hope in God.

**Scripture**     Now, after he rose early on the first day of the week, he appeared first to Mary Magdalene, from whom he had cast out seven demons. She went out and told those who had been with him, while they were mourning and weeping.      Mark 16:9-10

**Meditation** For the garden is the only place there is,
but you will not find it
Until you have looked for it everywhere
and found it nowhere that is not a desert.
W. H. Auden, from *For the Time Being* [106]

*Through what desert experiences have we found God's garden?*

**Prayers**     Merciful God, you have not abandoned us to
the grave.
**Guide us with your steadfast love.**
In your presence there is fullness of joy.
**Guide us with your steadfast love.**

*Here, the people may add particular intercessions or thanksgivings.*

You send us into the world to tell the story of your
divine mercy.
**Guide us with your steadfast love.**

### Lord's Prayer

**Prayer** Jesus, strong deliverer and our lover, as you sent
Mary Magdalene to tell the good news of your
resurrection, so fill and embolden us with your love
that we may be your faithful witnesses in the world
today. In your name we pray. **Amen.**

**Going Out** Alleluia! Come to us, O risen Lord,
**and enliven us with your eternal love. Alleluia!**

# Forgiveness

*Vespers*     (Traditional hour: evening/end of the day)

*As we turn on lamps at dusk, we greet the evening by welcoming God to abide with us anew.*

**Opening**     Alleluia! By death, Christ tramples death.
**On those in the tombs, he bestows new life. Alleluia!**

**Prayer**     God of victory over death, your Son revealed
himself again and again to convince his followers of
his glorious resurrection: Grant that we may know
his risen presence, in love obediently feed his sheep
and care for the lambs of his flock, until we join the
hosts of heaven in worshiping you and praising the
one who is worthy of blessing and honor, glory and
power, for ever and ever. **Amen.** [107]

**Praise**     *Light of the World*     *Phos hilaron* [108]

Light of the world, in grace and beauty,
Mirror of God's eternal face,
Transparent flame of love's free duty,
You bring salvation to our race.
Now, as we see the lights of evening,
We raise our voice in hymns of praise;
Worthy are you of endless blessing,
Sun of our night, lamp of our days.

**Scripture**     Jesus said to Simon Peter, "Simon, son of John, do
you love me?" He said to him, "Yes, Lord;
you know that I love you." Jesus said to him,
"Tend my sheep."                    John 21:16

**Meditation** The future will be different if we make the present different. Peter Maurin [109]

*How will we make the future different by caring for others now?*

**Confession** *During the joyful season of Easter, the Confession of Sin is omitted in order for worship to emphasize the celebration of redemption and new life that are characteristic of this season.*

## Assurance of Pardon

We know that our old self was crucified with Christ so that the body of sin might be destroyed, and we might no longer be enslaved to sin. ... So you must consider yourselves dead to sin and alive to God in Christ Jesus. Romans 6:6, 11

**Prayers** Jesus, in your life we receive life:
 **Raise us to the new life of grace.**
You look with compassion on our human failings:
 **Raise us to the new life of grace.**
We proclaim the hope of your resurrection as we
 offer you these prayers:

*Here, the people may add particular intercessions or thanksgivings.*

You make us bearers of hope in a world of suffering
 and despair:
 **Raise us to the new life of grace.**

## Lord's Prayer

**Prayer**       Lord Jesus, stay with us, for evening is at hand
and the day is past; be our companion in the way,
kindle our hearts, and awaken hope, that we may
know you as you are revealed in Scripture and the
breaking of the bread. Grant this for the sake of
your love. **Amen.** [110]

**Going Out**   Alleluia! By death, Christ tramples death.
**On those in the tombs, he bestows new life.**
**Alleluia!**

# Trust

*Compline*    (Traditional hour: night/bedtime)

*We sum up this day with a bedtime prayer to examine our conscience and offer our actions to God.*

**Opening**    Alleluia! May God, who raised Jesus from the dead, **grant us a peaceful night and a perfect end. Alleluia!**

**Prayer**    God, you sent your Son into the world that we might live through him: May we abide in his risen life so that we may love one another as he first loved us, and know the fullness of joy. **Amen.**

**Praise**    *Psalm 113* [111]
   Hallelujah! Give praise, you servants of God;
      praise the Name of the Most High.
   Let God's Name be blest,
      from this time forth for evermore.
   From the rising of the sun to its going down
      let God's holy Name be praised.
   God is high above all nations,
      and God's glory above the heavens.
   Who is like our God, who sits enthroned on high,
      but stoops to behold the heavens and the earth?
   God takes up the weak out of the dust
      and lifts up the poor from the ashes.
   To set them up on high,
      with the rulers of the people.
   God makes the woman of a childless house
      to be a joyful mother of children.

**Scripture**   May the God of peace, who brought back from the dead our Lord Jesus, the great shepherd of the sheep, by the blood of the eternal covenant, make you complete in everything good so that you may do his will, working among us that which is pleasing in his sight, through Jesus Christ, to whom be the glory for ever and ever.   Hebrews 13:20-21

**Meditation**   A characteristic of the great saints is their power of levity. The angels fly because they can take themselves lightly.   G. K. Chesterton [112]

*As this day closes, what burdens can we lay down?*

**Prayers**   O God of peace, in our disappointments and in our triumphs,
**Let us rest secure in your loving arms.**
In our certainty and in our confusion,
**Let all people rest secure in your loving arms.**

*Here, the people may add particular intercessions or thanksgivings.*

As we await a new day,
**Let all creation rest secure in your loving arms.**

**Lord's Prayer**

**Prayer**   All shall be Amen and Alleluia.
We shall rest and we shall see.
    We shall see and we shall know.
We shall know and we shall love.
    We shall love and we shall praise.
Behold our end, which is no end. **Amen.**
   Saint Augustine [113]

**Closing**   Alleluia! May God, who raised Jesus from the dead, **grant us a peaceful night and a perfect end.**
   **Alleluia!**

# Watch

*Vigils*        (Traditional hour: late night)

*Like nuns and monks at prayer, we can listen in the stillness of the night to hear God's call.*

**Opening**        Alleluia! O risen Christ,
            **watch with me. Alleluia!**

**Scripture**        Jesus came and stood among them and said,
            "Peace be with you."                    John 20:19b

**Meditation** *How will I accept Christ's peace this night?*

**Prayer**        All praise to thee, my God, this night
            for all the blessings of the light;
            keep me, O keep me, King of kings,
            beneath thine own almighty wings. [114]

**Closing**        Alleluia! O risen Christ,
            **watch with me. Alleluia!**

# Ordinary Time: Creation

The Season after Pentecost is not actually a season with a single common focus, but is simply the weeks between the Day of Pentecost and the First Sunday of Advent. It is often called "Ordinary Time." These weeks hold both the slower pace and peaceful quality of summer months and the quicker pace and flurry of activity in the early fall. These are our "ordinary" days, in which we live the Christian faith in our daily lives.

During these weeks, as the liturgical scholar Leonel Mitchell puts it, we celebrate "the time in which we actually live — the period between the Pentecost and the Second Advent." Two thousand years after the first Pentecost, the church still lives in this "in between" time before the fulfillment of time in Christ's second coming. You might also hear these weeks called "the long, green season," referring both to the green color of the vestments and altar hangings for these weeks as well as to the summertime of year in which many of the weeks fall in the northern hemisphere.

After Pentecost we settle into the growing season, nourishing the seeds planted at Easter and putting down roots in our faith.

# Praise

*Lauds*     (Traditional hour: dawn/waking up)

Laudate omnes, gentes, laudate Dominum!
*[Sing praises, all people, sing praises to the Lord!]*
*We greet the new day by praising the Creator*
*(the ancient name for this hour, Lauds, means "praise").*

**Opening**     This is the day that the Lord has made;
        **I will rejoice and be glad in it.**

**Scripture**     O Lord, how manifold are your works!     Psalm 104:27

**Meditation**   *How will I use the gift of this new day?*
        *How will I notice the glory of creation?*

**Prayer**     Many and great, O God, are thy works,
        maker of earth and sky;
        thy hands have set the heavens with stars;
        thy fingers spread the mountains and plains.
        Lo, at thy word the waters were formed;
        deep seas obey thy voice.

        Grant unto us communion with thee,
        thou star-abiding one;
        come unto us and dwell with us;
        with thee are found the gifts of life.
        Bless us with life that has no end,
        eternal life with thee.

        *Wakantanka taku nitawa*
        *tankaya qaota;*
        *mahpiya kin eyehnake ca,*
        *makakin he duowanca.*
        *Mniowanca sbeya wanke cin,*
        *hena ovakihi.*

    Many and Great "Dakota Hymn" / Lacquiparle by Joseph r. Renville (1942)
      paraphrased by R. Phillip Frazier (1929). Alt. *Hymnal* 1982, Hymn 385.

**Going Out**   This is the day that the Lord has made;
        **I will rejoice and be glad in it.**

# Discernment

*Prime*        (Traditional hour: morning/start of the day)

*As we begin the day, we focus on our calling to live faithfully, for who knows what today holds?*

**Opening**        Holy God, you are always with us.
                **Open our eyes to your presence.**

**Prayer**        God of faithful surprises, throughout the ages you have made known your love and power in unexpected ways and places: May we daily perceive the joy and wonder of your abiding presence and offer our lives in gratitude for our redemption. **Amen.** [115]

**Praise**        *Benedicite Omnia Opera*

                All you works of God, bless your creator;
                **praise her and glorify her for ever.**

                Let the wide earth bless the creator;
                let the arching heavens bless the creator;
                let the whole body of God bless the creator;
                **praise her and glorify her for ever.**

                You returning daylight, bless your creator;
                twilight and shadows, bless your creator;
                embracing darkness, bless your creator;
                **praise her and glorify her for ever.**

                Let all who live and grow and breathe
                bless our creator,
                **praise her and glorify her for ever.**

                                                Janet Morley [116]

**Scripture**        I am the vine, you are the branches. Those who abide in me and I in them bear much fruit because, apart from me, you can do nothing. You did not choose me, but I chose you. And I appointed you to go and bear fruit, fruit that will last.        John 15:5, 16a

**Meditation** People say that walking on water is a miracle, but to me, walking peacefully on the earth is the real miracle.                                    Thich Nhat Hanh [117]

*How will we walk in peace today?*

**Affirmation**

We believe in God, the creator of all life and beauty,
>   who blesses our journey.

We believe in Jesus Christ,
>   who lived as a friend and saviour to all he met
>       as he travelled,
and who ate and laughed, wept and celebrated
>       with them in love.

We believe in the Holy Spirit,
>   who rides on the gentle breeze,
>   who strengthens our bindings, and
>   who offers hope eternal.

We believe in the church,
>   which stands open to all travellers,
>   and bears witness to the everlasting love of God. [118]

**Prayers** As we turn to the tasks before us this day,
**Fill us, gracious Lord.**
In making faithful choices, great and small,
**Guide us, gracious Lord.**
As we seek to notice and serve those in need,
**Teach us, gracious Lord.**

*Here, the people may add particular intercessions
or thanksgivings.*

As we offer our lives to you,
**Hear us, gracious Lord.**
With our hearts ready to serve,
**Accompany us, gracious Lord.**

## Lord's Prayer

**Prayer**      Generous Giver, you pour forth your extravagant bounty without measure upon your whole creation: Teach us such generosity, that the fruits of our spirits and the works of our hands may build your commonwealth of blessing. **Amen.** [119]

**Going Out**  Holy God, you are always with us.
**Open our eyes to your presence.**

# Wisdom

*Terce*     (Traditional hour: mid-morning)

*Having asked for direction and guidance, we pray now to equip ourselves properly for the journey ahead.*

**Opening**      Let all who desire wisdom
         **walk in love.**

**Prayer**      Holy Lord, giver of all wisdom: Set for us this day
         the banquet of your word; invite us to feast on
         the genius and beauty all around us. Then, turn
         us in humility toward the poor, the oppressed and
         the weak; we ask this in the name of Jesus, who is
         Wisdom for ever and ever. **Amen.** [120]

**Praise**      *A Song of Pilgrimage*   (Ecclesiasticus 51:13-16, 20b-22) [121]

Before I ventured forth, even while I was very
       young, *
   I sought wisdom openly in my prayer.
In the forecourts of the temple I asked for her, *
   and I will seek her to the end.
From first blossom to early fruit, *
   she has been the delight of my heart.
My foot has kept firmly to the true path, *
   diligently from my youth have I pursued her.
I inclined my ear a little and received her; *
   I found for myself much wisdom and
       became adept in her.
To the one who gives me wisdom will I give glory, *
   for I have resolved to live according to her way.
From the beginning I gained courage from her; *
   therefore I will not be forsaken.
In my inmost being, I have been stirred to seek her; *
   therefore have I gained a good possession.
As my reward, the Almighty has given me
       the gift of language,*
   and with it will I offer praise to God.

Scripture     But the wisdom from above is first pure, then
              peaceable, gentle, willing to yield, full of mercy
              and good fruits, without a trace of partiality or
              hypocrisy. And a harvest of righteousness is sown in
              peace for those who make peace.          James 3:17-18

Meditation    Focus on Wisdom and do not be distracted. Watch
              the patterns of creation, and you will awaken to
              grace and tranquility.          Proverbs 3:19-22 [122]

              *How will we remain focused today so as to receive
              wisdom from creation?*

Prayers       O God, in peace, you have prepared our path for today.
              **Help us to trace it in peace.**
              If we speak,
              **Remove lies from our lips.**
              If we are hungry,
              **Rid us of complaint.**
              If we have plenty,
              **Flatten the pride in us.**
              We offer these prayers of our hearts to your
                  wise guidance:

              *Here, the people may add particular intercessions
              or thanksgivings.*

              May we pass through the day, calling on you,
              **O Lord, who knows no other Lord. Amen.** [123]

Lord's Prayer

Prayer        Holy One, in love you created us and called it
              good: Grant us the deep wisdom of your love that,
              wherever this day leads, our lives may remain
              rooted in your goodness; through Jesus Christ, our
              Lord. **Amen.**

Going Out     Let all who desire wisdom
              **walk in love.**

# Perseverance and Renewal

*Sext*       (Traditional hour: mid-day)

*As we pause to feed our bodies in the middle of the day, we pause also to feed our souls by vowing again to live faithfully.*

**Opening**      God's power, working in us,
                  **does more than we imagine: Glory to God!**

**Prayer**       Creating God, your reign of love makes all things new: Plant seeds of confidence and gladness in our hearts so that, trusting in your word, we may live no longer for ourselves but for him who died and was raised for us, Jesus Christ, our Lord. **Amen.** [124]

**Praise**       *For the Beauty of the Earth*

      For the beauty of the earth,
      For the beauty of the skies,
      For the love which from our birth
      Over and around us lies:
      Christ our God, to thee we raise
      This our sacrifice of praise.

      For the beauty of each hour,
      Of the day and of the night,
      Hill and vale and tree and flower,
      Sun and moon and stars of light:
      Christ, our God, to thee we raise
      This our sacrifice of praise.

Words: Folliot Sandford Pierpont (1835-1917)

**Scripture**    So let us not grow weary in doing what is right, for we will reap at harvest-time if we do not give up. So then, whenever we have an opportunity, let us work for the good of all, and especially for those of the family of faith.                    Galatians 6:9-10

**Meditation** Care ... rests upon genuine religion. Care allows creatures to escape our explanations into their actual presence and their essential mystery. In taking care of our fellow creatures, we acknowledge that they are not ours; we acknowledge that they belong to an order and harmony of which we ourselves are parts. To answer to the perpetual crisis of our presence in this abounding and dangerous world, we have only the perpetual obligation of care.                    Wendell Berry [125]

*At this hour, how is God calling us to care for creation?*

**Prayers**    O God, whose Spirit moved upon the waters,
we remember those who live in lands of drought
            or flood,
      whose harvest is not-enough or not-at-all.
**Today, they sow in tears:**
**soon, may they reap with shouts of joy.**

We remember those whose water supply is polluted
            by negligence or need,
      those to whom water brings disease, poisoning
            or radiation,
      whose gift of life is cursed by death.
**Today, they sow in tears:**
**soon, may they reap with shouts of joy.**

We remember ourselves:
> We devastate the waters and the fruits of the earth,
> and we are unwilling to form one circle
> with our brothers and sisters around the world.

*Here, the people may add particular intercessions
or thanksgivings.*

And we ask, Merciful Creator,
> **to shed their tears**
> **that soon we may all reap with shouts of joy.** [126]

**Lord's Prayer**

**Prayer**    Source of life and blessing,
of garden, orchard, field:
Root us in obedience to you
and nourish us by your ever-flowing Spirit
that, perceiving only the good we might do,
our lives may be fruitful,
our labour productive,
and our service useful,
in communion with Jesus, our brother. **Amen.** [127]

**Going Out**   God's power, working in us,
**does more than we imagine: Glory to God!**

# Love

*As shadows lengthen, we are filled by the day's encounters; now,
more than ever, we accept the depth and breadth of God's grace.*

**Opening**     As you have loved us,
              **may we love one another.**

**Prayer**      O Tree of Calvary, send your roots deep into my
              soul. Gather together my frailties — my soiled
              heart, my sandy instability and my muddy desires
              — and entwine them with the strong roots of your
              arboreal love. **Amen.** [128]

**Praise**      Lord God, we praise you for those riches of
                        our creation
                    that we will never see:
              For stars whose light will never reach the earth;
              For species of living things that were born,
                    that flourished and perished
                    before humankind appeared in the world;
              For patterns and colors in the flowers,
                    which only insect eyes are able to see;
              For strange, high music
                    that humans can never hear.
              Lord God, you see everything that you have made
                    and behold that it is very good.        Anonymous [129]

**Scripture**   I give you a new commandment, that you love one
              another. Just as I have loved you, you also should
              love one another. By this everyone will know that
              you are my disciples, if you have love for one
              another.                                    John 13:34-35

**Meditation**  Isn't that what friendship is all about: giving to each other the gift of our belovedness?

Henri Nouwen [130]

*Where do we need to offer and receive the gift of our belovedness? How can we treat the earth as beloved?*

**Prayers**  As the day lengthens, O Christ,
**Teach us to walk in your love.**
While we strive to be faithful in word and deed,
**Teach us to love one another.**
While we live as part of your creation,
**Teach us to love this good earth.**
While we offer our prayers this hour:

*Here, the people may add particular intercessions or thanksgivings.*

With grateful hearts,
**Teach us to trust in your love.**

**Lord's Prayer**

**Prayer**  Gracious Lord, the air sings with songs of glory, water flashes silver with creation, and the forests bloom with leaves for healing nations: May your light and love fill our hearts and souls and minds, that we may share your love with the world. **Amen.** [131]

**Going Out**  As you have loved us,
**may we love one another.**

# Forgiveness

*Vespers*     (Traditional hour: evening/end of the day)

*As we turn on lamps at dusk, we greet the evening by welcoming God to abide with us anew.*

**Opening**     If anyone is in Christ,
**there is a new creation.**

**Prayer**     Creating God, your reign of love makes all things new: Plant seeds of confidence and gladness in our hearts, so that, trusting your word, we may live no longer for ourselves but for him who died and was raised for us, Jesus Christ our Lord. **Amen.** [132]

**Praise**     *Doxology* [133]

May none of God's wonderful works keep silence,
        night or morning.
Bright stars, high mountains, the depths of the seas,
        sources of rushing rivers:
May all these break into song as we sing
        to Creator, Saviour and Holy Spirit.
May all the angels in the heavens reply:
Amen! Amen! Amen!
Power, praise, honor and eternal glory to God,
        the only giver of grace.
Amen! Amen! Amen!                    Anonymous (third century)

**Scripture**     So if anyone is in Christ, there is a new creation: everything old has passed away; see, everything has become new! All this is from God, who reconciled us through Christ and has given us the ministry of reconciliation.                    2 Corinthians 5:17-18

**Meditation**  We should be clear about what happens when we destroy the living forms of this planet.
The first consequence is that we destroy modes of divine presence.                                        Thomas Berry [134]

*What will we do today to preserve God's work in creation?*

**Confession**  We confess
that we have considered the earth to be our own,
believing God gave us dominion and, thus, absolute control over it.
We affirm that
"the earth is the LORD's and all that is in it,
for he has founded it on the seas and established it on the rivers." (Psalm 24:1-2)
We repent.
We know we need to change our understanding of creation,
taking our share of responsibility for its care and protection.
We believe
that the Spirit, God's recreating power,
is active in us and in the world.
God, Creator of all,
may humankind be freed from greed, which is destroying the earth;
and may your courageous churches take up causes against the forces
that threaten life.
Amen. [135]

**Assurance of Pardon**

> God does not deal with us according to our sins,
> nor repay us by the measure of our failings.
> As vast as the distance from one end of creation to
> another,
> God's love for us is even greater.
> As far as east is from west,
> from greater than this distance does God remove
> our sin from us.
> **Thanks be to God.** [136]

**Prayers**   Holy One, we praise you for the wonders of
> your creation:
> **Make us joyful and faithful stewards.**
> As the day grows long,
> **Bless us with the gift of laying down our burdens.**
> And not ours only:
> **Help us lift the weights we have placed on
> others and on your creation.**
> We offer these prayers of our hearts:
>
> *Here, the people may add particular intercessions
> or thanksgivings.*
>
> Create in us, again and always, your heart of grace.
> **May we rest on the sure foundation of your love.**

**Lord's Prayer**

**Prayer**   Give us strength to understand and eyes to see;
teach us to walk the soft earth as related to all that
lives. **Amen.** [137]

**Going Out**   If anyone is in Christ,
**there is a new creation.**

# Trust

*Compline*   (Traditional hour: night/bedtime)

*We sum up this day with a bedtime prayer to examine our conscience and offer our actions to God.*

**Opening**   The Lord almighty grant us a peaceful night
**and a perfect end. Amen.**

**Prayer**   God our desire, whose coming we look for, but
whose arrival is unexpected:
Here in the darkness make us urgent to greet you,
and open yourself to our longing that we may be
known by you through Jesus Christ, Amen. [138]

**Praise**   *Lifetime Psalm* [139]

Praise my soul, our good Lord.
Sing songs to God's name,
for God has brought my life
into fresh waters when I was thirsty.
God has fed me with the Bread of Life
when I was starving.
God has sustained me along all my days
and never has put me to shame.
Praise my soul, our good Lord,
for such abundant goodness.

**Scripture**   Blessed are those who trust in the Lord, whose trust
is the Lord. They shall be like a tree planted by
water, sending out its roots by the stream. It shall
not fear when heat comes, and its leaves shall stay
green; in the year of drought, it is not anxious, and
it does not cease to bear fruit.          Jeremiah 17:7-8

**Meditation** Fish cannot drown in water, birds cannot sink in air, gold cannot perish in the refiner's fire. This has God given to all creatures: to foster and seek their own nature. Mechthild of Magdeburg (13<sup>th</sup> century)

*What has God given us today to help us be more fully ourselves?*

**Prayer** Creator God,
you call us to love and serve you with body, mind, and spirit
through loving your creation and our sisters and brothers.
Open our hearts in compassion and receive these petitions
on behalf of the needs of the church and the world.

*Here, the people may add particular intercessions or thanksgivings.*

## Lord's Prayer

**Prayer** Holy One, you planted us by living water, that we might be rooted in righteousness. You call us to be holy as you are holy. Assured of your love, help us cast aside all fear, so that we may love our neighbours as ourselves. **Amen.** [140]

**Closing** The Lord almighty grant us a peaceful night **and a perfect end. Amen.**

# Watch

*Vigils*        (Traditional hour: late night)

*Like nuns and monks at prayer, we can listen in the stillness of the night to hear God's call.*

**Opening**        All creation longs for grace:
                   **I wait in hope.**

**Scripture**      Be still, then, and know that I am God;
                   I will be exalted among the nations;
                   I will be exalted in the earth.        Psalm 46:11 (BCP)

**Meditation**     *How will I be still and trusting this night?*

**Prayers**        Hidden God, ever present to me,
                       may I now be present to you,
                           attentive to your every word,
                           attuned to your inspirations,
                           alert to your touch.
                   Empty me that I may be filled with you alone.
                   **Amen.** [141]

**Closing**        All creation longs for grace:
                   **I wait in hope.**

# Ordinary Time: Rest

# Praise

*Lauds* (Traditional hour: dawn/waking up)

Laudate, omnes gentes, laudate Dominum!
*[Sing praises, all people, Sing praises to the Lord!]*
*We greet the new day by praising the Creator*
*(the ancient name for this hour, Lauds, means "praise").*

**Opening** I begin this day with joy:
**God is good.**

**Scripture** God saw everything that God had made, and, indeed, it was very good. Genesis 1:31

**Meditation** *How will I receive God's goodness today?*

**Prayer** Holy Creator, help me to embrace this day with open arms and to share your good gifts with gladness and generosity. **Amen.**

**Going Out** I begin this day with joy:
**God is good.**

# Discernment

*Prime*     (Traditional hour: morning/start of the day)

*As we begin the day, we focus on our calling to live faithfully, for who knows what today holds?*

**Opening**     We are called in the morning
              **to turn our hearts to you.**

**Prayer**      God grant me the serenity to accept the things I
              cannot change; courage to change the things I can;
              and wisdom to know the difference. Living one day
              at a time; enjoying one moment at a time; accepting
              hardships as the pathway to peace; taking, as Jesus
              did, this sinful world as it is, not as I would have it;
              trusting, O God, that you will make all things right
              if I surrender to your will; that I may be reasonably
              happy in this life and supremely happy with you for
              ever in the next. **Amen.** [142]

**Praise**      Rejoice, people of God!
              Celebrate the life within you,
              and Christ's presence in your midst!

              Our eyes shall be opened!
              The presence will have new meaning,
              and the future will be bright with hope.

              Rejoice, people of God!
              Bow your heads before the One
              who is our wisdom and our strength.

              We place ourselves before our God,
              that we may be touched and cleansed
              by the power of God's Spirit. [143]

**Scripture**    Consider the lilies, how they grow: they neither toil nor spin; yet I tell you, even Solomon in all his glory was not clothed like one of these.    Luke 12:27

**Meditation**  The final fruitfulness of work is actually found by choosing and living its exact opposite — the cessation of work — or the Sabbath rest. Unless approximately one-seventh of life is also ceasing from work, putting spaces, paragraphs, and parentheses around my efforts, work always becomes compulsive, addictive, driven, unconscious, and actually counter-productive for the self and for those around us. We also need not to work.    Richard Rohr [144]

*Today, how will we cease from work?*

**Affirmation**

> We believe in God, who loves us and wants us to love each other.
> This is our God.
>
> We believe in Jesus, who cared for children and held them in his arms.
> He wanted a world where everyone could live together in peace.
> This is Jesus Christ.
>
> We believe in the Holy Spirit, who keeps working with us until everything is good and true.
> This is the Holy Spirit.
>
> We can be the church, which reminds people of God because we love each other.
> This we believe. Amen. [145]

**Prayers**    As we begin our day,
                **Give us your peace.**
                As we pause this morning,
                **Give us your peace.**
                As we do the work you have given us to do,
                **Give us your peace.**
                For all places of need in this world,
                **Give us your peace.**
                In trusting you, O God, to care for your children,
                **Give us your peace.**
                As we seek wholeness,
                **Give us your peace.**

                *Here, the people may add particular intercessions
                or thanksgivings.*

                As we reflect on your presence,
                **Let us be peace for others.**

**Lord's Prayer**

**Prayer**     Holy One, we are too often blinded by trivial
                matters. Lord, may our attention be diverted now
                from these things, and may we become as little
                children, trusting and seeking with love to cross
                bridges that we have not crossed in the past.
                **Amen.** [146]

**Going Out**  We are called in the morning
                **to turn our hearts to you.**

# Wisdom

*Terce*          (Traditional hour: mid-morning)

*Having asked for direction and guidance, we pray now to equip ourselves properly for the journey ahead.*

**Opening**     Listen and hear:
                **Be still and know.**

**Prayer**      O Holy Wisdom, direct us on your path. Make
                us worthy of your teachings and open our hearts
                to accept your embrace, that we may serve you in
                peace and grace. **Amen.**

**Praise**      *A Song of Pilgrimage*
                (Ecclesiasticus 51:13-16, 20b-22; metrical paraphrase) [147]

                Even when young, I prayed for wisdom's grace;
                in temple courts I sought her day and night,
                and I will seek her to the very end;
                she is my heart's delight.

                My foot has firmly walked the path of truth;
                with diligence, I followed her design.
                My ear was open to receive her words;
                now wisdom's skill is mine.

                Glory to one who gives me wisdom's prize;
                I vowed to live according to her way.
                She gave me courage from the very start;
                she will not let me stray.

                Something within my being has been stirred;
                my seeking brought a gift beyond compare:
                the gift of language loosed my halting tongue;
                God's praise is now my prayer.

                                    Words: Patricia B. Clark (b. 1938)

**Scripture**   Resting your thoughts on Her [Wisdom] — this is perfect understanding. Staying mindful of Her — this is perfect calm. She embraces those who are ready for Her, revealing Herself in the midst of their travels, meeting them in every thought.

Wisdom of Solomon 6:15-16

**Meditation**   in the new light
of each day's questions,
I am never prepared.
Today, again, I have nothing
to offer but a handful
of old prayers, worn down
by the relentless abrasion
of doubt, and a fragment
of dream that plays on in my head
only half remembered. Still,
the doves coo and circle
through the pines
as they do when I pass
each morning. Their sorrow
is so nearly human, it rings
sweet with regret. By dusk,
the trees will bow down, and I, too, will
make my appeal, will find
again your mercy,
your solace.                Elizabeth Drescher [148]

*How will we embrace Wisdom's light and love this morning?*

| Prayers | Holy Wisdom, we rest in your goodness: |
|---|---|
| | **Guide us with your grace.** |
| | For your Church we ask: |
| | **Guide us with your grace.** |
| | For our world we ask: |
| | **Guide us with your grace.** |
| | For our communities we ask: |
| | **Guide us with your grace.** |
| | And for ourselves: When we speak, |
| | **Guide us with your grace.** |
| | When we desire, |
| | **Guide us with your grace.** |
| | When we are afraid, |
| | **Guide us with your grace.** |
| | We offer these prayers of our hearts to you: |

*Here, the people may add particular intercessions or thanksgivings.*

As we journey this day,
**Guide us with your grace.**

**Lord's Prayer**

Prayer  Grant us, Lord, your wisdom as we face the questions of this day. Reveal to us the faithful path, and, O Holy Wisdom, may we make you our heart's illumination. **Amen.**

Going Out  Listen and hear:
**Be still and know.**

# Perseverance and Renewal

*Sext*        (Traditional hour: mid-day)

*As we pause to feed our bodies in the middle of the day, we pause also to feed our souls by vowing again to live faithfully.*

**Opening**      My grace is sufficient for you,
          **for power is made perfect in weakness.**

**Prayer**      Grant us, O God, not to be anxious about earthly things but to love things heavenly and, even now, while we are placed among things that are passing away, to hold fast to those that shall endure; through Christ our Lord, **Amen.** [149]

**Praise**      *Peace before us*

          Peace before us, peace behind us,
          Peace under our feet.
          Peace within us, peace over us,
          Let all around us be peace.

          Light before us, light behind us,
          Light under our feet.
          Light within us, light over us,
          Let all around us be light.

          Love before us, love behind us,
          Love under our feet.
          Love within us, love over us,
          Let all around us be love.

          Christ before us, Christ behind us,
          Christ under our feet.
          Christ within us, Christ over us,
          Let all around us be Christ.
                    Words: David Haas (based on a Navaho prayer) [150]

**Scripture**  When I came to you, brothers and sisters, I did not come proclaiming the mystery of God to you in lofty words or wisdom. My speech and my proclamation were not with the persuasiveness of wisdom but with a demonstration of the Spirit and of power, so that your faith might rest not on human wisdom but on the power of God.

I Corinthians 2:1,4-5

**Meditation**  Whenever I am weak, then I am strong.

St. Paul (2 Corinthians 12:10b)

*How do we find strength manifested in weakness?*

**Prayers**  In our daily tasks,
**God surrounds us.**
In our successes and failures,
**God surrounds us.**
In our joys and sorrows,
**God surrounds us.**
With the healing of our world,
**God surrounds us.**
We pray for all who celebrate, or seek, or need
God's love:

*Here, the people may add particular intercessions or thanksgivings.*

As we continue our day,
**God surrounds us in hope.**

**Lord's Prayer**

**Prayer**  O Holy One, we keep still; we listen.
We hear you say, "I am your strength."
And we say to you, "You are our redeemer."
**Amen.** [151]

**Going Out**  My grace is sufficient for you,
**for power is made perfect in weakness.**

# Love

*As shadows lengthen, we are filled by the day's encounters; now, more than ever, we accept the depth and breadth of God's grace.*

**Opening**     What we offer is enough:
          **God's love covers all.**

**Prayer**      Creator and lover of our souls: Teach us to release
          our burdens and accept your love.
          May your love be the deepest reality of our lives,
          and may we offer real love to others. **Amen.**

**Praise**      *A Song of God's Love*  (I John 4:7-11) [152]

          Beloved, let us love one another, *
               for love is of God.
          Whoever does not love does not know God, *
               for God is love.
          In this, the love of God was revealed among us, *
               that God sent his only Son into the world,
               so that we might live through Jesus Christ.
          In this is love, not that we loved God but that
                    God loved us *
               and sent his Son that sins might be forgiven.
          Beloved, since God loved us so much, *
               we ought also to love one another.
          For if we love one another, God abides in us, *
               and God's love will be perfected in us.

| Scripture | Come to me, all of you who are weary and are carrying heavy burdens, and I will give you rest. Take my yoke upon you, and learn from me, for I am gentle and humble in heart, and you will find rest for your souls. |

Matthew 11:28

| Meditation | "Wasn't I Real before?" asked the little Rabbit. "You were Real to the Boy," the Fairy said, "because he loved you. Now you shall be Real to everyone." |

Margery Williams, *The Velveteen Rabbit* [153]

*What does it take to offer real love to another?*
*How shall we do that today?*

| Prayers | May the longtime sun shine upon us.
**God's love is in us.**
May God's love shine on all people.
**God's love is all in all.**
May all people know God's love.
**God's love fills us all.** |

*Here, the people may add particular intercessions or thanksgivings.*

May the pure light of God's love
**Lead us to love others.**

### Lord's Prayer

| Prayer | O love of God, how strong and true! Eternal,
    and yet ever new;
uncomprehended and unbought, beyond all
    knowledge and all thought:
bless us with your love, that, in loving others we
    may honor you. **Amen.** [154] |

| Going Out | What we offer is enough:
**God's love covers all.** |

148

# Forgiveness

*Vespers*    (Traditional hour: evening/end of the day)

*As we turn on lamps at dusk, we greet the evening by welcoming God to abide with us anew.*

**Opening**    Holy One, lift our burdens,
**for your yoke is easy.**

**Prayer**    O God, as the showers renew the earth, bathe us in your healing power. Stretch out your hand, that we may live and know that you alone are God, in whose faithfulness we have life all our days. **Amen.** [155]

**Praise**    *A Song of Our True Nature*  (Julian of Norwich) [156]

Christ revealed our frailty and our falling, *
    our trespasses and our humiliations.
Christ also revealed his blessed power, *
    his blessed wisdom and love.
He protects us as tenderly and as sweetly when
        we are in greatest need; *
    he raises us in spirit
    and turns everything to glory and joy without
    ending.

God is the ground and the substance, the very
        essence of nature; *
    God is the true father and mother of natures.
We are all bound to God by nature, *
    and we are all bound to God by grace.
And this grace is for all the world, *
    because it is our precious mother, Christ.
For this fair nature was prepared by Christ for
        the honor and nobility of all, *
    and for the joy and bliss of salvation.

| Scripture | Little children, let us love, not in word or speech, but in truth and action. By this we will know that we are from the truth and will reassure our hearts before him whenever our hearts condemn us; for God is greater than our hearts, and he knows everything. |
| --- | --- |
| | I John 3:19-20 |

Meditation   Where there is no love, put love, and you will draw
love out.                          St. John of the Cross [157]
*Where have we neglected to put love? Where do we
ask that love be drawn from us?*

Confession   **Most loving God,**
            **we confess that we have not loved**
            **in thought, word, or deed.**
            **We have not loved you or our neighbours**
               **or ourselves.**
            **We are sorry.**
            **Remind us that you love us unconditionally**
            **and help us to rest in your love.** [158]

**Assurance of Pardon**
            Loving God, have mercy on us, forgive us for
            forgetting to love, and renew our ability to give and
            receive love in all that we do. **Amen.** [159]

Prayers     Gracious Lord, whenever we err,
            **Fill our hearts with your love.**
            When we wound or are wounded,
            **Fill our hearts with your love.**
            When tempted to judge,
            **Fill our hearts with your love.**
            Wherever there is hurt, loss, or despair,
            **Fill our world with your love.**

            *Here, the people may add particular intercessions
            or thanksgivings.*

Make us faithful instruments of your peace.
**May we fill our world with your love.**

**Lord's Prayer**

Prayer        Lord, make me an instrument of your peace. Where there is hatred, let me sow love; where there is injury, pardon; where there is doubt, faith; where there is despair, hope; where there is darkness, light; and where there is sadness, joy. O Divine Master, grant that I may not so much seek to be consoled as to console; to be understood as to understand; to be loved as to love. For it is in giving that we receive; it is in pardoning that we are pardoned; and it is in dying that we are born to eternal life. **Amen.** [160]

Going Out   Holy One, lift our burdens,
**for your yoke is easy.**

# Trust

*Compline*    (Traditional hour: night/bedtime)

*We sum up this day with a bedtime prayer to examine our conscience and offer our actions to God.*

**Opening**     As a loving mother comforts her child,
                  **so I will comfort you.**

**Prayer**     O God, at the setting of the sun, we place our trust in you. As the night draws near, we give thanks for your presence with us. Help us entrust our lives to you with the delight and confidence of one who loves and is beloved. Through Jesus, our faithful Saviour. **Amen.**

**Praise**     *Leaning on the Everlasting Arms*

What a fellowship, what a joy divine,
Leaning on the everlasting arms;
What a blessedness, what a peace is mine,
Leaning on the everlasting arms.

> *Refrain*
> Leaning, leaning,
> safe and secure from all alarms;
> Leaning, leaning,
> Leaning on the everlasting arms.

O how sweet to walk in this pilgrim way,
Leaning on the everlasting arms;
O how bright the path grows from day to day,
Leaning on the everlasting arms.     *Refrain*

What have I to dread, what have I to fear,
Leaning on the everlasting arms;
I have blessed peace with my Lord so near,
Leaning on the everlasting arms.     *Refrain*

Words: Elisha A. Hoffman (1839-1929)

| | |
|---|---|
| Scripture | My beloved speaks and says to me: "Arise, my love, my fair one, and come away; for now the winter is past, the rain is over and gone. The flowers appear on the earth; the time of singing has come, and the voice of the turtledove is heard in our land. The fig tree puts forth its figs, and the vines are in blossom; they give forth fragrance. Arise my love, my fair one, and come away." *Song of Solomon 2:10-13* |

Meditation The measure of love is to love without measure.

*Attributed to Augustine*

*What "measure" will we release in order to embrace God's love this hour?*

Prayers The cares of our hearts
**We entrust to you, O God.**
The needs of your Church
**We entrust to you, O God.**
The wounds of the world
**We entrust to you, O God.**
The hopes we carry
**We entrust to you, O God.**
The deep desire for peace
**We entrust to you, O God.**

*Here, the people may add particular intercessions or thanksgivings.*

With all our lives and all our holy longings
**We praise you and trust your love for us,
O Lover of our souls. Amen.**

**Lord's Prayer**

Prayer      Gracious God, support us all the day long, until the
shadows lengthen, and the evening comes, and the
busy world is hushed, and the fever of life is over,
and our work is done. Then in your mercy, grant us
a safe lodging, and a holy rest, and peace at the last.
**Amen.** [161]

Closing     As a loving mother comforts her child,
**so I will comfort you.**

# Watch

*Vigils*        (Traditional hour: late night)

*Like nuns and monks at prayer, we can listen in the stillness of the night to hear God's call.*

**Opening**    God of love,
               **when I rest, I feel you near.**

**Scripture**  I will dwell in your house forever;
               I will take refuge under the cover of your wings.
                                                    Psalm 61:4

**Meditation** *Consider the promise that God's love*
               *is ever with you.*
               *How does it feel to rest in that care?*

**Prayers**    Spirit of comfort and longing,
               enfold my fear,
               unclothe my pride,
               unweave my thoughts,
               uncomplicate my heart,
               and give me surrender:
               that I may tell my wounds,
               lay down my work,
               and greet the dark. **Amen.** [162]

**Closing**    God of love,
               **when I rest, I feel you near.**

# Appendix

## The Lord's Prayer

*Two translations of the Lord's Prayer are in use in The Episcopal Church today. The form on the left has been in use since the first American Prayer Book, adopted in 1789. The form on the right was produced during the 1970s by the ecumenical International Consultation on English Texts, which was convened to produce agreed versions of texts at a time when many churches in many countries were producing modern-language liturgies.*

Our Father, who art in heaven,
   hallowed be thy Name,
   thy kingdom come,
   thy will be done,
      on earth as it is in heaven.
Give us this day our daily bread.
And forgive us our trespasses,
  as we forgive those
   who trespass against us.
And lead us not into temptation,
  but deliver us from evil.
For thine is the kingdom,
  and the power, and the glory,
  for ever and ever. Amen.

Our Father in heaven,
   hallowed be your Name,
   your kingdom come,
   your will be done,
      on earth as in heaven.
Give us today our daily bread.
Forgive us our sins
  as we forgive those
   who sin against us.
Save us from the time of trial,
  and deliver us from evil.
For the kingdom, the power,
  and the glory are yours,
  now and for ever. Amen.

*In the earliest editions of the Book of Common Prayer (published in England during the sixteenth century), the Lord's Prayer ended with "deliver us from evil." It appears again this way in the services of Noonday Prayer and Compline in the 1979 Book of Common Prayer:*

Our Father, who art in heaven,
   hallowed be thy Name,
   thy kingdom come,
   thy will be done,
     on earth as it is in heaven.
Give us this day our daily bread.
And forgive us our trespasses,
   as we forgive those
    who trespass against us.
And lead us not into temptation,
   but deliver us from evil.

Our Father in heaven,
   hallowed be your Name,
   your kingdom come,
   your will be done,
     on earth as in heaven.
Give us today our daily bread.
Forgive us our sins
   as we forgive those
    who sin against us.
Save us from the time of trial,
   and deliver us from evil.

# Notes

## Advent

1 The seasonal introductions are taken and adapted from *Welcome to the Church Year: An Introduction to the Seasons of The Episcopal Church* by Vicki K. Black (Morehouse Publishing, 2004). Used by permission.

2 *The Message.*

3 Words: Charles Price, adapt., © 1982 Hope Publishing Company, Carol Stream, IL 60188. All rights reserved. Used by permission.

4 Sam Portaro, *Daysprings: Meditations for the Weekdays of Advent, Lent and Easter* (Boston: Cowley Publications, 2001), p. 6.

5 *Revised Common Lectionary Prayers*, alt., proposed by the Consultation on Common Texts (Minneapolis: Fortress Press, 2002), p. 31.

6 Canticle R, A Song of True Motherhood, Julian of Norwich, *Enriching Our Worship 1* (New York: Church Publishing Inc., 1998), p. 40.

7 Quoted in Robert Ellsberg, *All Saints: Daily Reflections on Saints, Prophets, and Witnesses for Our Time* (New York: Crossroad, 1997), p. 148.

8 Janet Morley, "Collect for 6 before Christmas," *All Desires Known* (exp. ed.) (Morehouse Press, 1992), p. 4.

9 *Revised Common Lectionary Prayers*, p. 34.

10 The Song of Mary (*Magnificat*), *Enriching Our Worship 1*, p. 27.

11 Wendell Berry, excerpted from "Manifesto: The Mad Farmer Liberation Front," in *Collected Poems: 1957-1982* (New York: North Point Press, 1985), p. 152.

12 *Revised Common Lectionary Prayers*, p. 34.

13 *Revised Common Lectionary Prayers*, p. 29.

14 Janet Morley, "Christmas 2," *All Desires Known*, p. 6.

15 Canticle P, *Enriching Our Worship 1*, pp. 38-39.

16 J. Philip Newell, *The Book of Creation: An Introduction to Celtic Spirituality*, pp. 11, 13. Copyright © 1999 by J. Philip Newell. Paulist Press, Inc., Mahwah, NJ. Reprinted by permission of Paulist Press, Inc. www.paulistpress.com.

17 The concluding stanza, "Make us holy," from Institute for Spirituality, CPSA, as found in *An African Prayer Book*, Desmond Tutu, ed. (New York: Doubleday, 1995), p. 80.

18 Janet Morley, "Advent 3," *All Desires Known*, p. 5.

19 Excerpted from The Song of Hannah, 1 Samuel 2:1-8, as found in *Enriching Our Worship I*, p. 31.

20 Marilyn Chandler McEntyre, "What to do in the darkness," as found in Holly W. Whitcom, *Seven Spiritual Gifts of Waiting* (Minneapolis: Augsburg Books, 2005), p. 38.

21 *Revised Common Lectionary Prayers*, p. 33 (alt.).

# Christmas

22 Order of St. Helena, The St. Helena Psalter (Church Publishing Inc., 2000).

23 *Revised Common Lectionary Prayers*, p. 38.

24 The Song of Mary, *Enriching Our Worship 1*, p. 27.

25 Miriam Therese Winter, from "A Psalm for Midwives," as found in *Midwives of an Unnamed Future: Spirituality for Women in Times of Unprecedented Change*, eds. Mary Ruth Broz and Barbara Flynn (Skokie, Ill.: ACTA Publications, 2006), p. 19.

26 Malinia Devananda, "A Woman's Creed," as found in *Lifting Women's Voices: Prayers to Change the World*, Margaret Rose, Jenny Te Paa, Jeanne Person and Abigail Nelson, eds. (New York: Domestic and Foreign Missionary Society/ Morehouse Publishing, 2009), pp. 371-372 (alt.).

27 Adapted from a prayer by Geoff Lowson/USPG, as found in *From Shore to Shore: Liturgies, Litanies and Prayers from Around the World* (London: Society for Promoting Christian Knowledge, 2003), p. 55. Prayer reproduced with permission from Us (United Society). www.weareUs.org.uk.

28 Janet Morley, "Collect for Christmas 1," *All Desires Known*, p. 6.

29 Dom Helder Camara (1909-1999) was Roman Catholic Archbishop of Recife, Brazil. Quoted in Robert Ellsberg's *All Saints: Daily Reflections on Saints, Prophets, and Witnesses for Our Time* (New York: Crossroads, 1997, 2004), p. 65

30 J. Philip Newell, *The Book of Creation* (Mahwah, N.J.: Paulist Press, 1999), p. 10.

31 Weiyu Zhiu and Ingren Wu, 1921; paraphrase: Kathleen Moody, © Kathleen Moody, as found in Chinese New Hymnal, © 1985 Chinese Christian Council. Permission sought.

32 From *The Way of Perfection* by Teresa of Avila, as found in *Midwives of an Unnamed Future*, p. 171.

33 Based on 1 John 3:18-4:21.

34 As quoted in *A Keeper of the Word: Selected Writings of William Stringfellow*, Bill Wylie-Kellermann, ed. (Grand Rapids, Mich.: Eedrmans, 1994), p. 314.

35 Adapted from Psalm 108.

36 Based on Luke 6:20-22.

37 Collect for the Second Sunday after Christmas Day, The Book of Common Prayer, p. 214.

38 Collect for the First Sunday after Christmas Day (alt.), The Book of Common Prayer, p. 213.

39 Dorothy Soelle, from *On Earth as in Heaven* (Westminster John Knox Press, 1983), p. 641.

40 *Revised Common Lectionary Prayers*, p. 46.

# Epiphany

41 Adapted from Joan Chittister, *Life Ablaze: a Woman's Novena* (Franklin. Wis.: Sheed & Ward, 2000), p. 34.

42 *Revised Common Lectionary Prayers*, p. 56.

43 Order of St. Helena, *St. Helena Psalter*, pp. 35-36

44  Terry Tempest Williams, "Refuge: An Unnatural History of Family and Place," as found in *The Sacred Earth: Writers on Nature and Spirit*, Jason Gardner, ed. (Novato, Ca.: New World Library, 1998), p. 42.

45  "A New Creed" from *Voices United: A Hymn and Worship Book* (Nashville: United Church Publishing House, 2007), p. 918. Used with permission. www.united-church.ca/beliefs/creed

46  Lancelot Andrewes (adapted).

47  "Canticle 26," The European Province of the Society of St Francis, *Celebrating Common Prayer* (London: Mowbray, 1995). Printed with permission from the Continuum International Publishing Company.

48  Book of Common Prayer copyright 2004 Representative Body of the Church of Ireland.

49  As printed in *Canticles of the Earth: Celebrating the Presence of God in Nature*, F. Lynn Bachleda, ed. (Chicago: Loyola Press, 2004), p. 3.

50  *Revised Common Lectionary Prayers*, p. 56.

51  Order of Saint Helena, *Saint Helena Breviary* (New York: Church Publishing, 2006), p. 10.

52  Thomas Merton, "at the corner of Fourth and Walnut," a journal entry on Merton's mystical experience in Louisville, Ky., as quoted in *All Saints: Daily Reflections on Saints, Prophets, and Witnesses for Our Time*, Robert Ellsberg, ed., p. 539.

53  *Revised Common Lectionary Prayers*, p. 66.

54  "Many Are the Light Beams," from *Wonder, Love, and Praise*, #794: Anders Frostenson, © AF-Foundation Hymns and Song, Verbum, Stockholm (original), Pablo D. Sosa © (translation).

55  Adapted from Richard Meux Benson, *Benedictus Dominus* (London: JT Hayes, 1870), p. 48.

56  *Revised Common Lectionary Prayers*, p. 61.

57  From the service of Evening Prayer, The Book of Common Prayer, p. 120.

58  By Denise Levertov, from *Breathing The Water*, copyright ©1987 by Denise Levertov. Reprinted by permission of New Directions Publishing Corp.

59  Collect for Compline, The Book of Common Prayer, p. 133.

60  Order of St. Helena, *St. Helena Psalter*.

61  Antiphon for Compline, The Book of Common Prayer, p. 134.

# Lent

62  Order of St. Helena, *St. Helena Psalter*.

63  Theophilus of Antioch, *Three Books to Autolychus*, I, 7, cited in Olivier Clement, *The Roots of Christian Mysticism,* trans. T. Berkeley (London: New City Press, 1993), 73.

64  From "Nicaragua," as found in *From Shore to Shore: Liturgies, Litanies and Prayers from Around the World,* Kate Wyles, ed. (London: SPCK, 2003), p. 92. Prayer reproduced with permission from Us (United Society). www.weareUs.org.uk

65  Erasmus of Rotterdam, 1466-1536.

66  Doris Atkers © 1953, renewed by Unichappell Music, Inc. (Rightson Music Publisher). International Copyright Secured. All Rights Reserved.

67  Oscar Romero, from *Through the Year with Oscar Romero* (Cincinnati, Ohio: St. Anthony Messenger Press, 2005), p. 56.

68  Prayer for Guidance, The Book of Common Prayer, p. 100.

69  *Music for Liturgy, 1999* (San Francisco: St. Gregory of Nyssa Episcopal Church), p. 20.

70  From *The Life of St. Anthony*, as found in *Following Christ: A Lenten Reader to Stretch Your Soul*, by Carmen Acevedo Butcher (Brewster, Mass.: Paraclete Press, 2010), p. 93.

71  Adapted from Janet Morley, *All Desires Known*, p. 73.

72  Sara Miles, based on Wisdom of Solomon 7, 2007.

73  *Revised Common Lectionary Prayers*, p. 88.

74  Canticle D, A Song of the Wilderness, *Enriching our Worship 1*, p. 32.

75  John Chrystostom, "Homily 50 on Matthew."

76  George Herbert, *Love (III)*.

77  Teresa of Avila, *Interior Castle*, trans. by the Benedictines of Stanbrook (1921), revised and edited by Fr. Benedict Zimmerman (1930), reprinted (2003) by Kessinger Publications, p. 109.

78  Adapted from *A Litany For The World We Live In*, quoted in *Bread of Tomorrow: Prayers for the Church Year*, Janet Morley, ed. (Maryknoll, NY: Orbis Books, 1992).

79  Canticle Q, *Enriching Our Worship 1*, p. 39.

80  Nan Merrill, *Psalms for Praying: An Invitation to Wholeness* (New York: The Continuum International Publishing Group, 2000), p. 211. Printed with permission from the Continuum International Publishing Company.

81  *Revised Common Lectionary Prayers*, p. 82.

82  Patricia B. Clark, 1995.

83  Li Po, *Endless River: Li Po and Tu Fu : A Friendship in Poetry*, Sam Hamill, trans. & ed. (Boston: Weatherhill, 1993). Permission sought.

84  Adapted from the Prayer of Saint Ephrem, c. 373.

85  2nd Prayer for the Presence of Christ, The Book of Common Prayer, p.124.

# Holy Week

86  *Revised Common Lectionary Prayers*, p. 96.

87  From *Wonder, Love, and Praise*, #734.

88  *Revised Common Lectionary Prayers*, p. 97.

89  Dorothy L. Sayers, *The Man Born to Be King*, © 1943.

90  Janet Morley, "Collect for Passion Sunday," *All Desires Known*, expanded ed. (Morehouse Publishing, 1992), p. 12.

91  Collect from Prayers for Noonday, The Book of Common Prayer, p. 107.

92  *Revised Common Lectionary Prayers*, p. 99.

93  Daniel Ladinsky, trans., *Love Poems from God: Twelve Sacred Voices from the East and West* (New York: Penguin Compass, 2002), p. 238.

94  *Revised Common Lectionary Prayers*, p. 98.

95 "As in That Upper Room," Words: Timothy Dudley-Smith, ©1993 Hope Publishing Company, Carol Stream, IL 60188. All rights reserved. Used by permission.

96 As found in *Bread and Wine: Readings for Lent and Easter* (Farmington, PA: The Plough Publishing House, 2003), p. 189.

97 Janet Morley, "Collect for Good Friday," *All Desires Known*, p. 13.

98 *Revised Common Lectionary Prayers*, p. 95.

99 *Revised Common Lectionary Prayers*, p. 102.

# Easter

100 Canticle K, *Enriching Our Worship 1*, p. 36.

101 Native American source, as cited in *From Shore to Shore*, p. 97. Prayer reproduced with permission from Us (United Society). www.weareUs.org.uk

102 Canticle A, *Enriching Our Worship 1*, p. 30.

103 As quoted in *All Saints: Daily Reflections on Saints, Prophets, and Witnesses for Our Time*, Robert Ellsberg, ed., p. 180.

104 *Revised Common Lectionary Prayers*, p. 112.

105 Canticle M, *Enriching Our Worship 1*, p. 37.

106 "For the Time Being," copyright © 1944 and renewed 1972 by W. H. Auden; from *W. H. Auden Collected Poems* by W. H. Auden. Used by permission of Random House, an imprint and division of Random House LLC. All rights reserved.

107 *Revised Common Lectionary Prayers*, p. 117.

108 *Enriching Our Worship 1*, p. 23.

109 As quoted in *All Saints: Daily Reflections on Saints, Prophets, and Witnesses for Our Time*, Robert Ellsberg, ed., p. 203.

110 A Collect for the Presence of Christ, The Book of Common Prayer, p. 124.

111 Order of St. Helena, *St. Helena Psalter*.

112 As quoted in *All Saints: Daily Reflections on Saints, Prophets, and Witnesses for Our Time*, Robert Ellsberg, ed., p. 235.

113 Saint Augustine, as found in *An African Prayer Book*, Desmond Tutu, ed., p. 33.

114 Thomas Ken, from *The Hymnal 1982*, p. 43.

# Ordinary Time: Creation

115 *Revised Common Lectionary Prayers*, p. 135.

116 Janet Morley, excerpted from *All Desires Known*, p. 37.

117 Thich Nhat Hahn, from *Love in Action: Writings on Nonviolent Social Change*, as found in *Canticles of the Earth: Celebrating the Presence of God in Nature*, F. Lynn Bachleda, ed. (Chicago: Loyola Press, 2004), p. 4. Words of Thich Nhat Hanh with permission of Parallax Press, Berkeley, California www.parallax.org

118 *From Shore to Shore*, p. 68. Prayer reproduced with permission from Us (United Society). www.weareUs.org.uk

119 *Revised Common Lectionary Prayers*, p. 170.

120 Adapted from J. Frank Henderson, *A Prayer Book for Remembering the Women* (Chicago: Liturgy Training Publications, 2001), p.119.

121 Canticle B, *Enriching our Worship 1*, p. 30.

122 Rabbi Rami Shapiro, trans. *The Divine Feminine in Biblical Wisdom Literature: Selections and Annotated & Explained* (Woodstock, Vermont: Skylight Paths Publishing, 2005), p. 169. Permission granted by SkyLight Paths Publishing, Woodstock, VT, www.skylightpaths.com

123 Adapted from "You have prepared in peace the path," as found in *An African Prayer Book* (New York: Doubleday, 1995), Desmond Tutu, ed., p. 119.

124 *Revised Common Lectionary Prayers*, p. 148.

125 Wendell Berry, from *Another Turn of the Crank*, as found in *The Sacred Earth: Writers on Nature and Spirit*, Jason Gardner, ed. (Novato, Ca.: New World Library, 1998), p. 115.

126 Adapted from a prayer written by Clare Amos/Methodist Church in the UK, as found in *From Shore to Shore: Liturgies, Litanies and Prayers from Around the World* (London: SPCK, 2003), p. 83. Prayer reproduced with permission from Us (United Society). www.weareUs.org.uk

127 *Revised Common Lectionary Prayers*, p. 85.

128 As found in *From Shore to Shore*, p. 79. Prayer reproduced with permission from Us (United Society). www.weareUs.org.uk

129 As found in *Canticles of the Earth: Celebrating the Presence of God in Nature*, F. Lynn Bachleda, ed. (Chicago: Loyola Press, 2004), p. 19.

130 Henri Nouwen, *Life of the Beloved: Spiritual Living in a Secular World* (New York: Crossroad Publishing, 1992), p. 30.

131 Adapted from *From Shore to Shore: Liturgies, Litanies and Prayers from Around the World* (London: SPCK, 2003), p. 98. Prayer reproduced with permission from Us (United Society). www.weareUs.org.uk

132 *Revised Common Lectionary Prayers*, p.148.

133 This version is slightly altered from *Canticles of the Earth: Celebrating the Presence of God in Nature*, F. Lynn Bachleda, ed. (Chicago: Loyola Press, 2004), p. 13.

134 Thomas Berry, as found in *The Sacred Earth: Writers on Nature and Spirit*, Jason Gardner, ed. (Novato, Ca.: New World Library, 1998), p. 121.

135 Adapted from the confession in "For the Healing of Creation: An order of service to celebrate creation," as found in *From Shore to Shore: Liturgies, Litanies and Prayers from Around the World* (London: SPCK, 2003), pp. 39-40. Prayer reproduced with permission from Us (United Society). www.weareUs.org.uk

136 Based on Psalm 103:10-12.

137 Native American prayer, as found in *From Shore to Shore: Liturgies, Litanies and Prayers from Around the World* (London: SPCK, 2003), p. 97. Prayer reproduced with permission from Us (United Society). www.weareUs.org.uk

138 Janet Morley, *All Desires Known*, p. 25.

139 Adapted from a prayer of the church in Uruguay, as found in *From Shore to Shore*, p. 91. Prayer reproduced with permission from Us (United Society). www.weareUs.org.uk

140 *Revised Common Lectionary Prayers*, p. 204.

141 Patricia B. Clark, *Women's Uncommon Prayers; Our Lives Revealed, Nurtured, Celebrated* (Morehouse Publishing, 2000), p. 222.

# Ordinary Time: Rest

142 Reinhold Neibuhr is credited as the author of the first form of this prayer, expanded by William Griffith Wilson, founder of Alcoholics Anonymous; known as "the serenity prayer," it is widely used by AA and other groups based on AA's 12-Step program (this version altered with inclusive language).

143 From the Methodist Church in Guatemala, as found in *From Shore to Shore*, p. 57. Prayer reproduced with permission from Us (United Society). www.weareUs.org.uk

144 *The Tasks Within the Tasks: A Spirituality of Work and Non-Work*, Richard Rohr, http://www.cacradicalgrace.org/resources/rg/2007/01_Oct-Dec/task.php

145 Prepared by children for the 1991 World Council of Churches' Assembly in Canberra, as found in *From Shore to Shore*, p. 67. Prayer reproduced with permission from Us (United Society). www.weareUs.org.uk

146 Adapted from statement by Samuel M. Tickle, as found in *Race and Prayer*, Malcolm Boyd, ed. (Harrisburg: Morehouse Publishing, 2003), p. 122.

147 Metrical paraphrase of Canticle B (*Enriching Our Worship*), text by Patricia B. Clark, as found in *Wonder, Love and Praise*, #906.

148 Elizabeth Drescher, "Morning Song," as found in *Women's Uncommon Prayers* (Harrisburg, Morehouse, 2000), p. 26.

149 Collect for Proper 20, The Book of Common Prayer (alt.), p. 234.

150 David Haas, based on a Navaho prayer. Copyright © 1987 by GIA Publications, Inc., 7404 S. Mason Ave., Chicago, IL 60638 www.giamusic.com 800.442.1358. All rights reserved. Used by permission.

151 Adapted from Sallie Cheavens Verette, "Silent Prayer," in *Women's Uncommon Prayers*, p. 224.

152 Canticle N, *Enriching Our Worship I*, pp. 37-38.

153 Margery Williams, *The Velveteen Rabbit* (New York: Doubleday, 1922, 1991), pp. 28-29.

154 "O love of God, how strong and true" (first phrase of this prayer), hymn text by Horatius Bonar (1808-1889), as found in *The Hymnal 1982*, pp. 455-456.

155 *Revised Common Lectionary Prayers*, p. 144.

156 Canticle S, *Enriching Our Worship 1*, p. 40.

157 "Letter 26, to Madre Maria de la Encarnacion, Segovia, July 6, 1591," in Kieran Kavanaugh and Otilio Rodriguez, trans., *The Collected Works of St. John of the Cross* (Washington, DC: ICS Publications, 1991), 760, http://www.icspublications.org/archives/others/cs6_3.html (accessed November 10, 2014).

158 Adapted from The Book of Common Prayer, p. 116.

159 Adapted from The Book of Common Prayer, p. 117.

160 Prayer of St. Francis of Assisi.

161 Collect for Evening, The Book of Common Prayer, p. 833.

162 Janet Morley, *All Desires Known*, p. 85.